LAND

OF THE

DINOSAURS

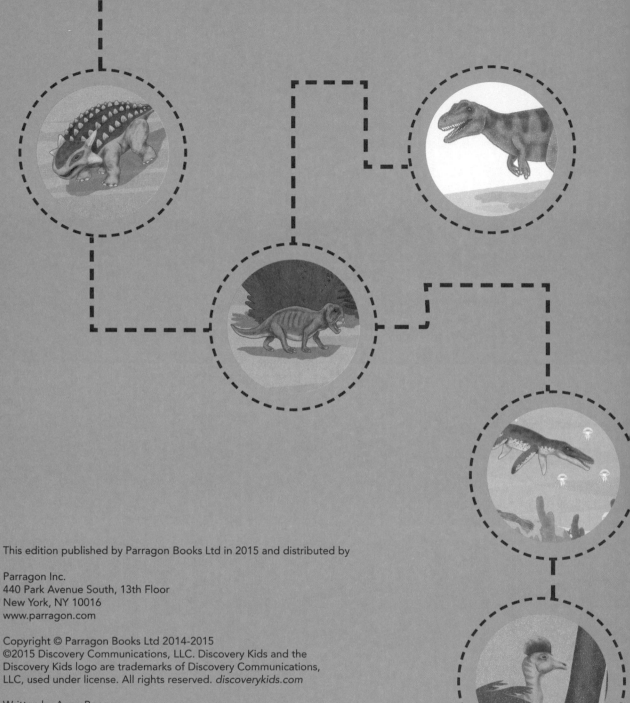

This edition published by Parragon Books Ltd in 2015 and distributed by

Parragon Inc.
440 Park Avenue South, 13th Floor
New York, NY 10016
www.parragon.com

Written by Anne Rooney
Illustrated by Adam Howling, Mar Ferrero
Consultant: Professor Michael Benton, FRS

ISBN 978-1-4723-9430-9

Printed in China

LAND

OF THE

DINOSAURS

PaRragon

Bath · New York · Cologne · Melbourne · Delhi
Hong Kong · Shenzhen · Singapore · Amsterdam

Contents

Meet the dinosaurs

Dinosaurs were some of the most amazing animals to have ever lived on our planet. Some were as tall as a four-story building and as long as four buses lined up end to end. Others were no bigger than a pet cat.

Dinosaurs were animals that roamed the Earth long before people existed!

Dinosaurs first appeared about 230 million years ago.

That's 80 times longer than humans have been around!

They went on to rule the world for 165 million years.

? **True or false quiz**

1. There were no people living during the time of the dinosaurs.

TRUE FALSE

2. All dinosaurs were huge!

TRUE FALSE

3. Dinosaurs lived during a time called the Messyzooic.

TRUE FALSE

Before the dinosaurs

To find out how dinosaurs came to rule our planet, you'll need to travel back in time. First, discover how life began and how the scene was set for the arrival of the dinosaurs.

Draw yourself looking out of the window of your time machine!

You're just in time to go back in time!

TIME TOURS

Jump into your time machine now. Your first stop is 4.5 billion years ago!

1 4.5 BILLION years ago

The Earth formed 4.5 billion years ago. For a billion years, it was a harsh and lifeless planet, shaken by huge earthquakes and violent volcanoes.

2 3.8 BILLION years ago

You need a microscope to see the first living things.

The Earth calmed down and oceans formed. Life began with tiny spots of blue-green algae in the sea. For three billion years, all living things were very small.

3 540 MILLION years ago

About 540 million years ago, everything changed. The seas filled with new life—first sponges and corals, then early types of shrimp and snail. Later, fish appeared.

4 440 MILLION years ago

The first plants grew on the land. Then some fish started to gulp air and wriggled out of the water. Over millions of years, they developed legs and moved onto land.

5 350 MILLION years ago

Life is really getting going on the land now!

These new land animals spread into the swamps and forests, and grew into different shapes and sizes. They ate the plants—and each other!

6 252 MILLION years ago

It's time to leave!!

Disaster! A massive volcanic eruption killed most living things on Earth. With the larger animals gone, there was plenty of space for the dinosaurs to take over.

Triassic tourist

Set your time machine to 220 million years ago, and start your dino safari during a time called the Triassic. This is when the first dinosaurs appeared on Earth!

The world was hot and dry. Forests of tall trees grew on the land, and ferns filled the space between them. There were no flowers, and no grass grew anywhere.

Dragonfly

There were not many different types of dinosaurs in the Triassic. They were also smaller than the dinosaurs that would develop later.

Zupaysaurus

Look! I've spotted our first dinosaur—Zupaysaurus, an early predator.

Dinosaurs shared the land with many other animals, including reptiles and giant insects.

Ischigualastia

Prehistoric dragonflies were as long as your forearm. Can you spot 10 buzzing around here?

• *Zupaysaurus* = ZOO-pay-SORE-us • *Ischigualastia* = ISCH-ee-gwal-astia

Welcome to Pangaea!

The world looked very different during the Triassic. All the land was joined together to form a giant supercontinent that we call Pangaea.

> Reptiles (including dinosaurs) and amphibians roamed this one huge landmass.

Eoraptor

> The land was surrounded by a vast ocean called Panthalassa. It was filled with fish, swimming reptiles, and other sea creatures.

Shonisaurus

To see what Pangaea looked like, color in the map to match the colored dots. Can you find the modern continents on your map?

- Africa
- North America
- South America
- Eurasia (Europe & Asia)
- Antarctica
- Australia

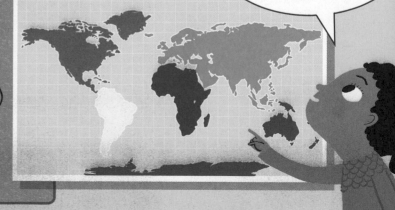

All the land in the world today was there in the Triassic period—it was just in different places!

Over millions of years, Pangaea eventually broke up into separate continents. These slowly drifted away from each other to form the world we know today.

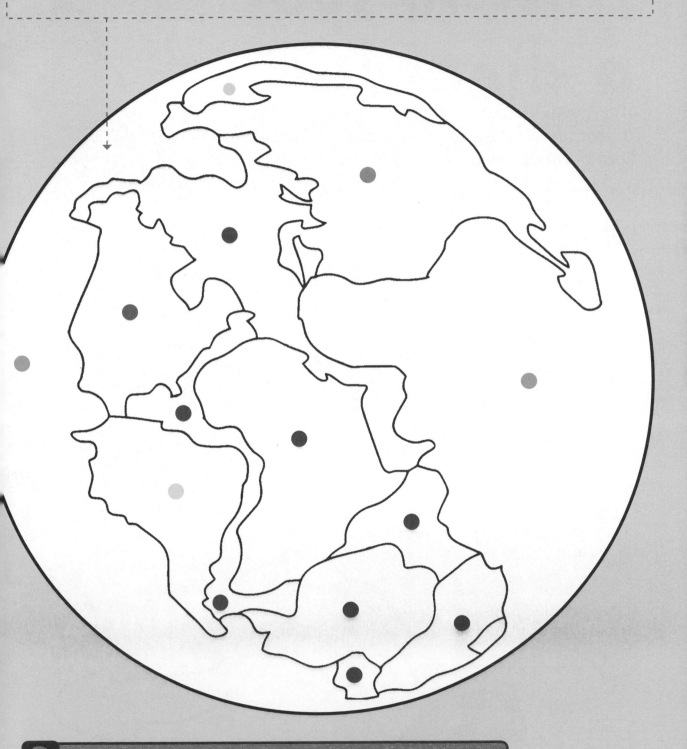

🛜 • **Pangaea** = Pan-JEE-uh   • **Panthalassa** = PAN-tha-lass-ah
• *Shonisaurus* = SHOW-nee-SORE-us   • *Eoraptor* = EE-oh-RAP-tor

How to spot a dinosaur

Now I know how to spot the dino!

The name "dinosaur" means Fearsome Lizard, but dinosaurs aren't really lizards at all. Use this handy field guide to help you spot dinosaurs on your trip.

1 Dinosaurs all lived on land. The prehistoric sea and skies were full of reptiles, but these animals were NOT dinosaurs.

Dinosaur ✔

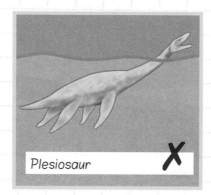

Plesiosaur ✘

Pterosaur ✘

2 Dinosaurs and lizards are both types of reptiles, but unlike lizards, dinosaurs walked (or ran) on legs that were directly under their bodies.

Having legs under their bodies meant that dinosaurs could grow larger than other reptiles.

Dinosaur

Lizard

3 Dinosaurs all had four limbs, though some walked on four legs and others on two.

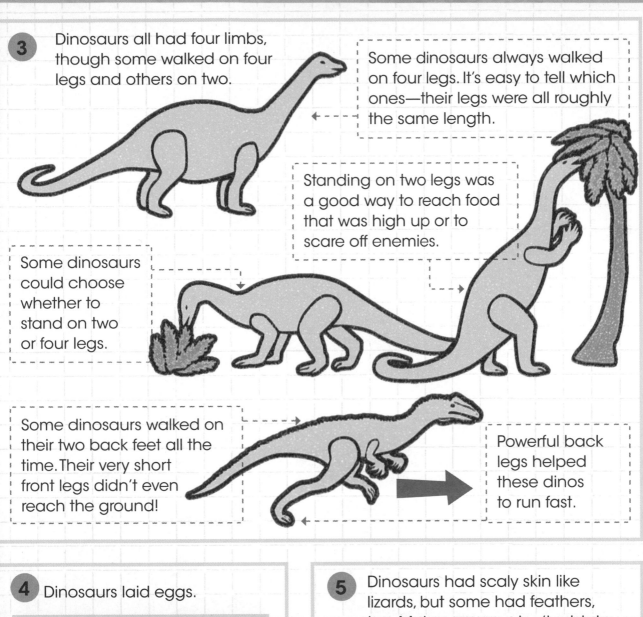

Some dinosaurs always walked on four legs. It's easy to tell which ones—their legs were all roughly the same length.

Standing on two legs was a good way to reach food that was high up or to scare off enemies.

Some dinosaurs could choose whether to stand on two or four legs.

Some dinosaurs walked on their two back feet all the time. Their very short front legs didn't even reach the ground!

Powerful back legs helped these dinos to run fast.

4 Dinosaurs laid eggs.

5 Dinosaurs had scaly skin like lizards, but some had feathers, too. Make sure you don't mistake these dinos for birds!

Early dinosaurs

The very first dinosaurs appeared 228 million years ago in an area of Pangaea that is South America today. Check out these tiny Triassic dinos on your field trip!

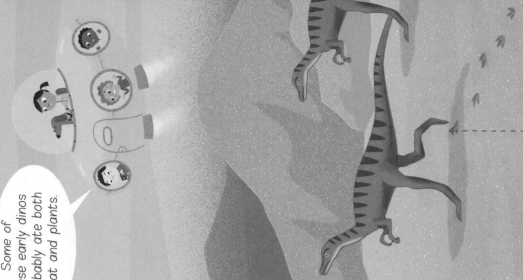

Some of these early dinos probably ate both meat and plants.

Panphagia could walk on two or four legs. Many later dinosaurs developed from this body shape, and some grew to be giants.

Eoraptor was about three feet long. It was small and nimble, running along on two legs. Three of its five fingers had large claws.

Staurikosaurus was a meat-eater. At about six feet in length, it was slightly bigger than *Eoraptor*. Like *Eoraptor*, it ran on strong back legs, using its long tail for balance.

Pisanosaurus was a plant-eater, about three feet long. It had a beak rather than lots of teeth. Lots of dinosaurs developed beaks later.

- *Panphagia* = pan-FAY-gee-uh • *Eoraptor* = EE-oh-RAP-tor
- *Staurikosaurus* = store-ik-oh-SORE-us • *Pisanosaurus* = pee-san-oh-SORE-us

Dinosaur dinners

Some dinosaurs were meat-eaters (carnivores), while others ate plants (herbivores). Other dinosaurs probably ate a bit of both.

Discover what each of these dinosaurs ate by finding a route that takes them to their dinner.

START

Liliensternus would have wanted to eat **Plateosaurus**. Many large meat-eating dinosaurs ate other dinosaurs.

A prehistoric dragonfly could be 25 inches wide—as big as a medium-sized modern bird!

FINISH

- *Liliensternus* = LIL-ee-en-STERN-us
- *Plateosaurus* = platt-ee-oh-SORE-us
- *Procompsognathus* = pro-comp-sog-NAYTH-us

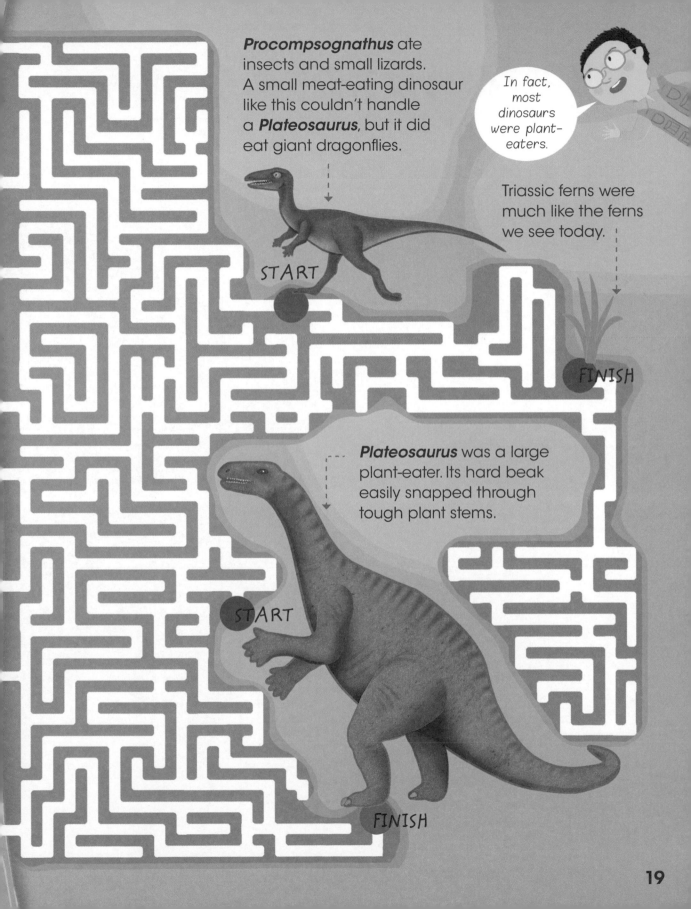

Procompsognathus ate insects and small lizards. A small meat-eating dinosaur like this couldn't handle a **Plateosaurus**, but it did eat giant dragonflies.

In fact, most dinosaurs were plant-eaters.

Triassic ferns were much like the ferns we see today.

START

FINISH

Plateosaurus was a large plant-eater. Its hard beak easily snapped through tough plant stems.

START

FINISH

Melanorosaurus

DINO FACT FILE

 Say: mel-uh-NOR-uh-SORE-us

 Meaning of name: black mountain lizard

 Length: 26 feet

 Diet: plants

 Lived: 228 to 210 million years ago

 Found in: South Africa

Melanorosaurus was the largest Triassic dinosaur!

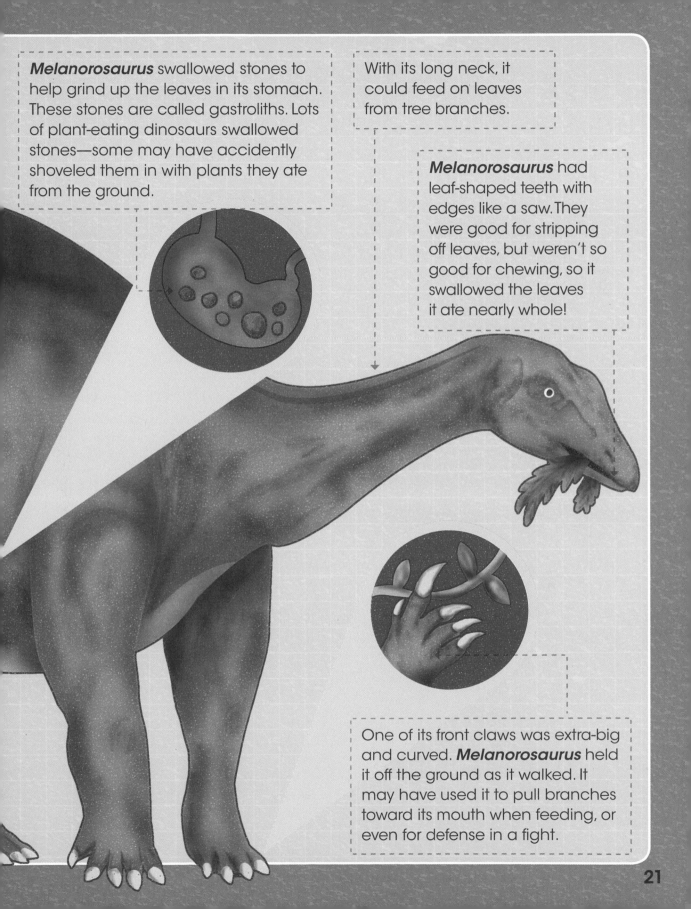

Melanorosaurus swallowed stones to help grind up the leaves in its stomach. These stones are called gastroliths. Lots of plant-eating dinosaurs swallowed stones—some may have accidently shoveled them in with plants they ate from the ground.

With its long neck, it could feed on leaves from tree branches.

Melanorosaurus had leaf-shaped teeth with edges like a saw. They were good for stripping off leaves, but weren't so good for chewing, so it swallowed the leaves it ate nearly whole!

One of its front claws was extra-big and curved. *Melanorosaurus* held it off the ground as it walked. It may have used it to pull branches toward its mouth when feeding, or even for defense in a fight.

Dino safari

The next stop for your time machine is 225 million years ago. Grab your binoculars and see if you can spot any dinosaurs. It may be harder than you think!

One way of hiding from hungry predators is to blend in with the background. This is called camouflage. Watch out, because being camouflaged can also help predators sneak up on prey.

I think I can see something moving in the ferns over there!

Some dinosaurs were probably camouflaged. Others may have been brightly colored.

How many hidden dinosaurs can you spot on your dino safari?

Scaly skin

Dinosaurs were covered in scales, just like crocodiles and snakes are today, but we don't know what colors most of them were. They might even have had spots and stripes, which make good camouflage patterns.

• *Euskelosaurus* = yoo-SKEE-loh-SORE-us

Roaming reptiles

Dinosaurs weren't the only kind of reptiles that lived on land in the Triassic. Take a look at some of the other reptiles that roamed around 228 million years ago.

Ischigualastia was a heavy and slow plant-eating reptile. Its strong beak snipped through tough roots and branches.

Tiny reptiles like **Probainognathus** had a hard time—lots of animals wanted to eat them! They had to move fast or creep into small spaces to stay safe.

- *Saurosuchus* = SORE-oh-SOO-kuss • *Probainognathus* = pro-BAY-no-NAY-thus
- *Hyperodapedon* = HIGH-per-oh-DAP-eh-DON • *Ischigualastia* = ISCH-ee-gwal-astia

Tiny *Probainognathus* was just four inches long. Can you find all six of them?

With dagger-shaped teeth, deadly **Saurosuchus** ate dinosaurs and other reptiles.

Although it looked a little like a modern-day crocodile, *Saurosuchus* lived on land and didn't go in the water.

Hyperodapedon's fangs made it look fierce, but it was actually a plant-eater that ate ferns.

Triassic seas

Dinosaurs all lived on the land, but the Triassic seas and oceans were also filled with living creatures, including sea reptiles and fish.

Even though they lived underwater, sea reptiles had to come to the surface to breathe.

Ichthyosaurs looked like fish, but were actually a group of sea reptiles that had developed from land reptiles. Over millions of years, they became more streamlined to help them move through the water.

Another group of marine reptiles were the placodonts. The name means "tablet teeth." They looked a little like present-day sea turtles.

Ichthyosaur means "fish lizard" —but these Triassic swimmers weren't fish or lizards!

Shonisaurus was an ichthyosaur with a long snout, but no teeth! It probably ate soft creatures such as squid.

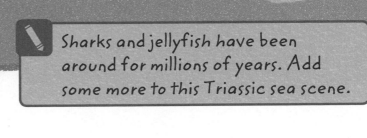

Sharks and jellyfish have been around for millions of years. Add some more to this Triassic sea scene.

Henodus was a placodont with a hard armored shell that helped it to sink to the bottom, where it shoveled up shellfish in its wide jaws.

Nothosaurs were a group of marine reptiles that caught their food in water, but came ashore to eat, like modern-day seals.

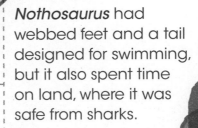

Nothosaurus had webbed feet and a tail designed for swimming, but it also spent time on land, where it was safe from sharks.

- *Shonisaurus* = SHOW-nee-SORE-us • *Henodus* = HEE-no-dus
- *Nothosaurus* = no-tho-SORE-us • *Ichthyosaurs* = ICK-thee-oh-sores

Coelophysis

DINO FACT FILE

 Say: seal-OH-fy-sis

 Meaning of name: hollow form

 Length: 9 feet

 Diet: meat

 Lived: 225 to 220 million years ago

 Found in: southwestern United States

Coelophysis was a fierce and fast-moving predator. Its long neck allowed it to quickly reach out and snap up prey.

Being lightweight helped **Coelophysis** to run fast. It ran upright on two legs, using its long, flexible tail to balance.

Coelophysis was somewhere between six to nine feet long, yet it weighed just 60 pounds—that's about the same as a medium-sized dog.

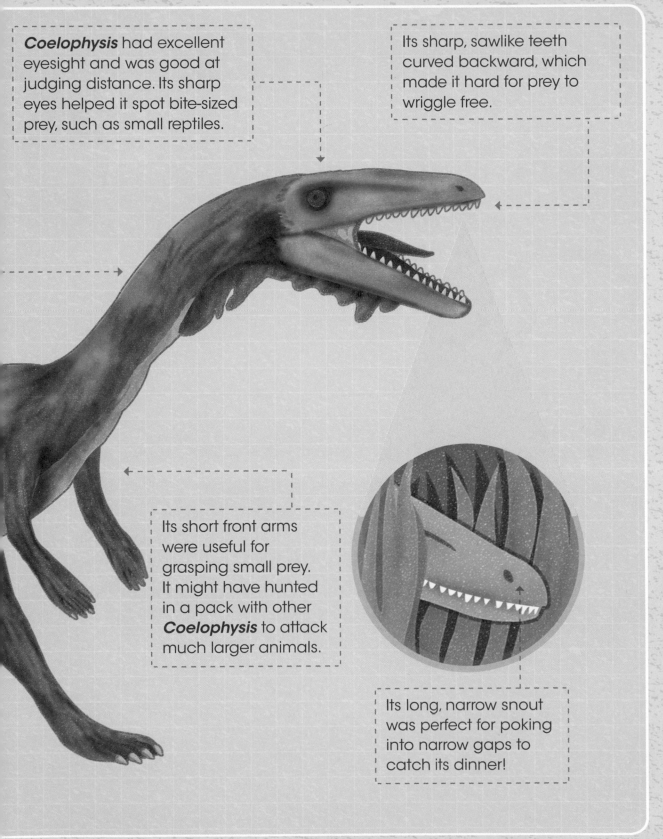

Coelophysis had excellent eyesight and was good at judging distance. Its sharp eyes helped it spot bite-sized prey, such as small reptiles.

Its sharp, sawlike teeth curved backward, which made it hard for prey to wriggle free.

Its short front arms were useful for grasping small prey. It might have hunted in a pack with other **Coelophysis** to attack much larger animals.

Its long, narrow snout was perfect for poking into narrow gaps to catch its dinner!

Draw Eoraptor

Eoraptor was one of the first dinosaurs to appear on Earth.

Oh no! A dinosaur just stepped on your camera! Worried that you might forget what dinos such as **Eoraptor** looked like when you get back home? No problem. Just draw one instead!

1

Use a pencil to draw a big oval on its side for the body and a smaller one above and to the left for the head.

2

Add in the neck and, then a long tail.

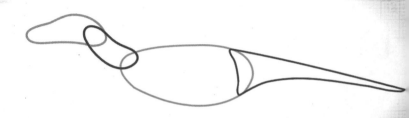

3

Sketch in the back legs and the short front arms with some roughly oval shapes.

4

Use circles to draw in the eyes. Then sketch in the clawed hands and feet as shown.

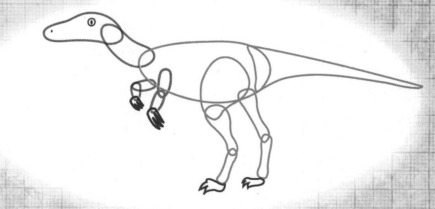

5

Finally, go over the outlines to make them thicker, and erase any guide lines. Then color in your *Eraptor*.

Its teeth seem designed for eating meat and plants, so it's likely that *Eoraptor* was an omnivore.

Soaring Pterosaurs

What are those flying creatures? Grab your binoculars and scan the Triassic skies. Dinosaurs couldn't fly—and there were no birds, so they must be pterosaurs!

Their wings were flaps of skin stretched between a very long fourth finger and their back feet. Other fingers stuck out as claws from the wing.

Pterosaurs were flying reptiles that could glide or flap their wings like a bird. They folded their wings up to walk on the ground when they landed.

Preondactylus had short wings and long rear legs, but it could still fly well. Like other pterosaurs at this time, it had a long, bony tail.

Eudimorphodon ate fish, plunging into the sea to snatch them from just below the surface. Its jaw was just over two inches long, but it had 110 teeth!

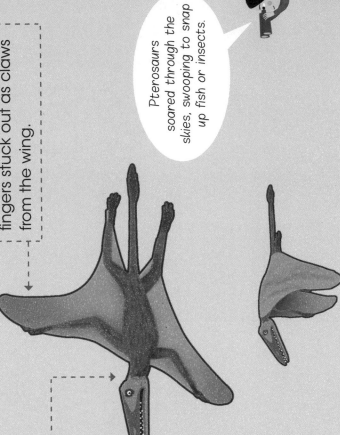

Pterosaurs soared through the skies, swooping to snap up fish or insects.

Carniadactylus looked similar to **Eudimorphodon**, but was much smaller. It ate worms and grubs, which it swallowed without chewing.

How many fish can you spot for *Eudimorphodon* to catch?

- Preondactylus = pre-on-DACK-tih-lus • Eudimorphodon = you-dye-MORE-fo-don
- Carniadactylus = car-nee-ah-DACK-till-us • Pterosaurs = tear-uh-SORES

Disaster!

Quick—get back in your time machine! Things aren't looking good . . . 201 million years ago, the world of the dinosaurs was shaken by a violent natural disaster.

Massive volcanic eruptions split the Earth apart and poured out scorching molten rock. On land this fiery lava devastated vast areas.

Plants struggled to survive, so there was less food for the animals that ate them. Many large plant-eating reptiles died.

The meat-eaters gobbled up the dying plant-eaters, but the feast was short-lived. Soon the meat-eaters went hungry and many died out.

The gases produced by the volcanoes heated up the land and the oceans. They also made acid rain, which killed plants.

The disaster struck the oceans, too, killing many sea plants and creatures.

Mass extinction

The volcanic eruptions that ended the Triassic killed half the types of plants and animals on the planet. They became extinct and were never seen again.

On land, many of the large reptiles and amphibians were wiped out. In the ocean, many types of sea creatures became extinct, too.

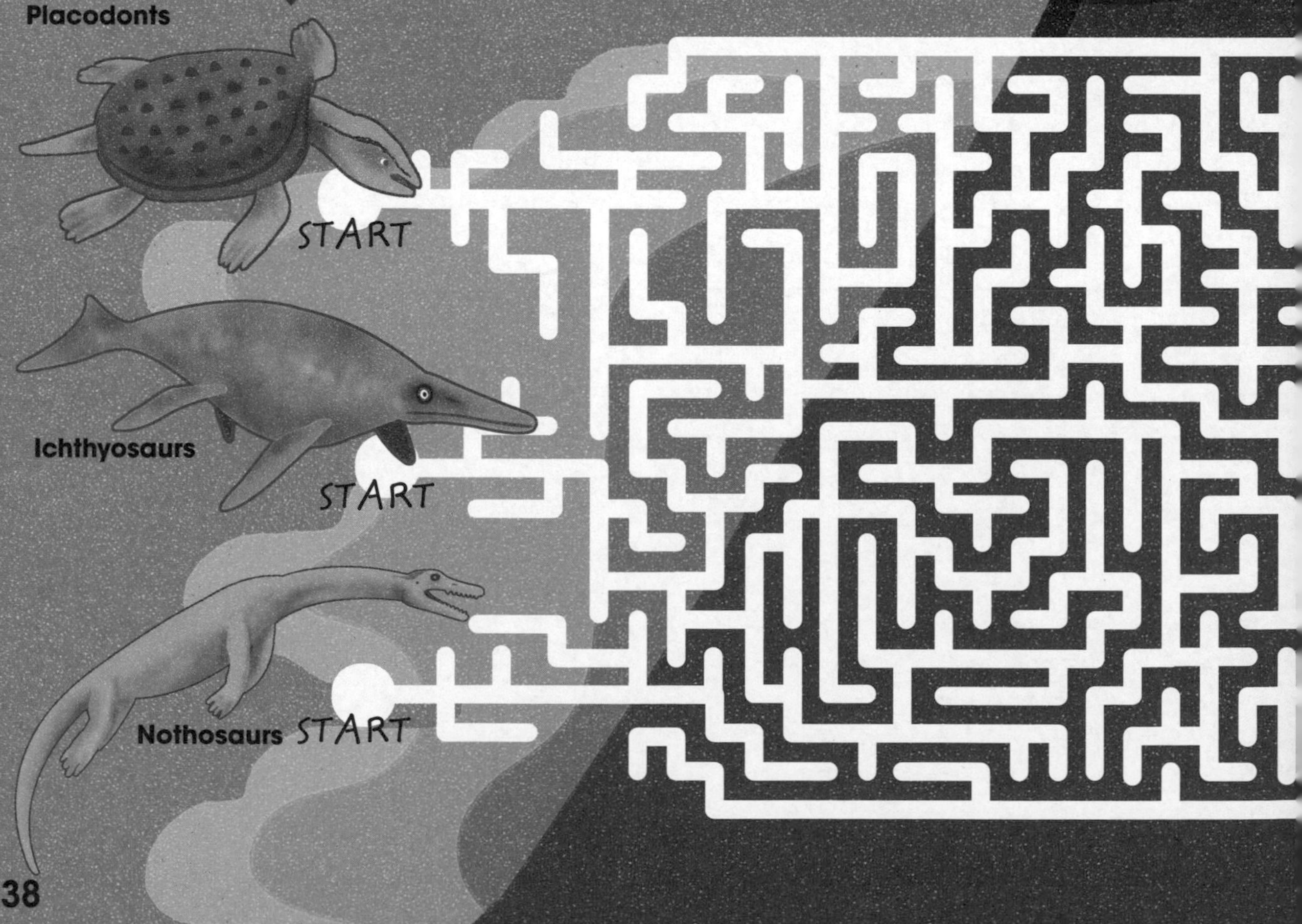

Placodonts

START

Ichthyosaurs

START

Nothosaurs START

39

Jurassic world

Fast-forward through time, from the Triassic period to the Jurassic. Many types of reptiles from the Triassic had vanished in the mass extinction, leaving dinosaurs to rule the world!

During the Jurassic period, 200 million years ago, the huge landmass of Pangaea started to break up. It split into two large continents: Gondwana and Laurasia.

Giraffatitan

LAURASIA

GONDWANA

✏️ Copy the *Giraffatitan* from Gondwana here.

The deserts shrank as rain forests and plants spread over large areas of the land. These provided food for the plant-eaters, who in turn were food for new meat-eating dinosaurs!

Dinosaurs could still cross between the two continents, so the types of dinosaur remained fairly similar across the world during the Jurassic.

However, they did get much bigger. The first of the sauropods, huge, plant-eating dinosaurs, appeared during the Jurassic. By the late Jurassic, giant sauropods, such as **Brachiosaurus** and **Giraffatitan**, roamed on land.

Brachiosaurus ———

 Copy the *Brachiosaurus* from Laurasia here.

Brachiosaurus weighed as much as 15 elephants!

 • Gondwana = GOND-wah-na • Laurasia = law-RAY-shuh
• *Brachiosaurus* = BRACK-ee-oh-sore-us • *Giraffatitan* = ji-RAFF-a-tie-tan

Dinosaur groups

In the Jurassic, new types of dinosaurs appeared. Many types of large reptiles had died out in the disaster at the end of the Triassic. This extinction left more food and living space for dinosaurs to develop.

Stegosaurus

Allosaurus

Gargoyleosaurus

Draw lines to match each Jurassic dino to its shadow and reveal the group it belongs to.

Experts group similar types of dinosaur together.

Ankylosaurs

A type of armored dinosaur. Ankylosaurs walked on four legs and had a deadly tail club.

Theropods

Dinosaurs that walked or ran on two legs, including many fierce meat-eating predators.

- *Allosaurus* = AL-oh-SORE-us
- *Stegosaurus* = STEG-uh-SORE-us
- *Gargoyleosaurus* = GAR-goyle-oh-SORE-us
- *Camptosaurus* = CAMP-tuh-SORE-us
- *Apatosaurus* = a-PAT-oh-SORE-us

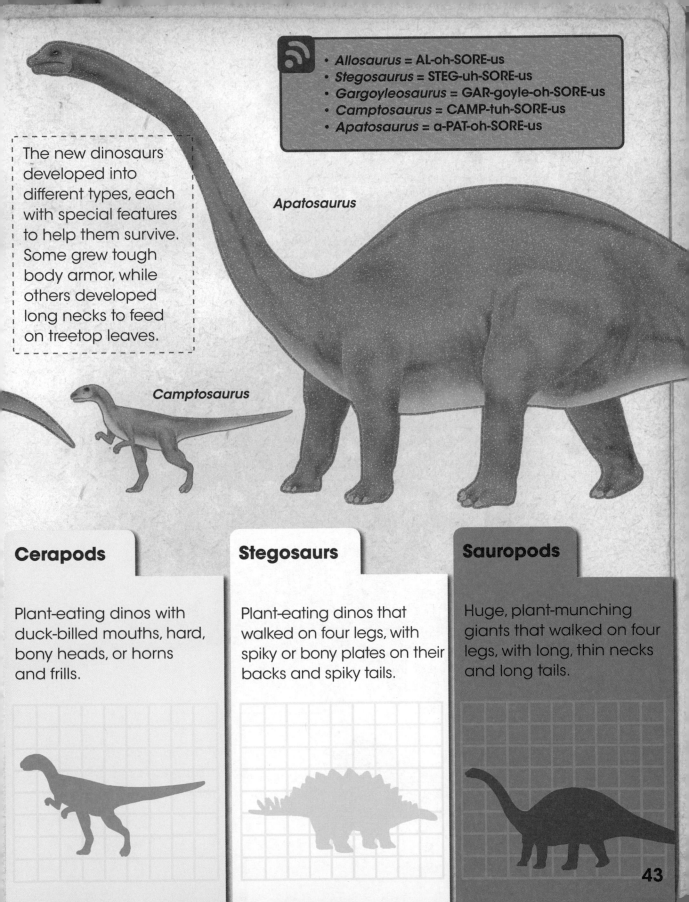

The new dinosaurs developed into different types, each with special features to help them survive. Some grew tough body armor, while others developed long necks to feed on treetop leaves.

Apatosaurus

Camptosaurus

Cerapods

Plant-eating dinos with duck-billed mouths, hard, bony heads, or horns and frills.

Stegosaurs

Plant-eating dinos that walked on four legs, with spiky or bony plates on their backs and spiky tails.

Sauropods

Huge, plant-munching giants that walked on four legs, with long, thin necks and long tails.

43

Size guide

Dinosaurs came in all shapes and sizes.
Some were among the largest land
creatures to have ever lived.
Others were as small as a
modern-day pigeon.

Apatosaurus
Length: 75 feet
Weight: 16 tons

Allosaurus
Length: 32 feet
Weight: 2.3 tons

Camptosaurus
Length: 16 feet
Weight: 1 ton

Amphicoelias was as long as four buses lined up end to end!

Amphicoelias
Length: 190 feet
Weight: 122 tons (the same as 20 elephants!)

The sauropods were the most supersized of the dinosaurs. **Amphicoelias** was the largest of these plant-eating giants.

Coelurus
Length: 6 feet
Weight: 44 pounds

Use a tape measure to figure out how many steps it takes you to walk one yard. Then walk 50 yards. That's the length of a big sauropod!

• *Amphicoelias* = AM-fih-SEE-lee-ass • *Coelurus* = SEE-loo-rus • *Sauropod* = SORE-o-pod

Dino tracking

It's time to follow the dino trail! When giants like **Diplodocus** stomped over soft ground, their feet made huge footprints. Other dinos made different shapes and sizes of footprints.

Lines of dinosaur footprints are called a trackway.

Trackways can tell us if a dinosaur walked on four legs or two.

Sauropod footprints can be more than three feet wide!

 • Ornithopods = oar-NITH-oh-PODS

Ornithopods

Ornithopod dinosaurs like **Iguanodon** could walk on four feet or two feet. Their footprints have three toes and a rounded shape.

Theropods

Theropods, such as **Allosaurus**, were bipedal, which means that they moved on two legs. They made more pointy three-toed footprints than ornithopods.

Sauropods

The biggest dino footprints were made by huge sauropods, such as **Diplodocus**. Herds left behind long trackways of rounded footprints.

47

Diplodocus

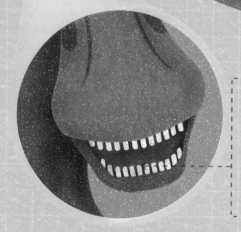

Diplodocus's head was tiny and its neck bones were hollow, which made them light. If the bones had been solid, its neck would have been too heavy to move around.

It used its long, thin teeth like a rake, dragging twigs through them to strip off the leaves.

DINO FACT FILE

 Say: di-PLOD-oh-kuss

 Meaning of name: double beam

 Length: 85 feet

 Diet: plants

 Lived: 155 to 145 million years ago

 Found in: United States

Diplodocus needed a huge stomach to break down all the leaves it ate. *Diplodocus* was so big, it needed to eat a lot of leaves every day.

Giant **Diplodocus** would have been able to reach the treetops without stretching. It was one of the plant-eating sauropods, a group that contained the largest of the dinosaurs.

To defend itself, **Diplodocus** could crack its long tail like a whip. The tip of its tail could reach a speed of 800 miles per hour!

Pooey!

Diplodocus cracked its tail fast enough to make a loud boom like a supersonic aircraft!

Because **Diplodocus** ate a lot, it also had a lot of waste material to get rid of and made the biggest dinosaur poops.

49

Growing up fast

It might sound unlikely, but even Jurassic giants like **Diplodocus** started small. Take a look at how a tiny baby **Diplodocus** grew up!

Hatchling

A **Diplodocus** egg was the largest egg EVER! It was roughly the same size as a football.

Baby

After just a week, the hatchlings doubled in weight. Soon after, the baby **Diplodocus** would increase in weight by four pounds a day—the same weight as two bags of sugar.

Compared to the size of Diplodocus's mom, the eggs were tiny!

Hatchlings were small and could easily be snapped up by predators. They grew up without their parents and probably lived in groups. They kept safe by hiding in places where big dinosaurs couldn't fit.

Teenager

When fully grown, a **Diplodocus** would have weighed a thousand times as much as when it hatched.

A young **Diplodocus** ate ferns, moss, and other low-growing plants almost all the time. By the time it was a teenager, it was gaining two tons a year—about eleven pounds a day!

You really are growing UP!

Hatch a baby dino by doodling some cracks on this egg. Then add a baby *Diplodocus*'s head poking out.

Big eater

A big plant-eating dinosaur needed a BIG dinner! To feed a pet *Diplodocus,* you would need 10,000 bags of salad every day!

Most dinosaurs ate plants and would have grazed over a large area. A smaller amount of meat-eating dinosaurs then preyed on the plant-eaters for their dinner.

So eating your greens really does make you big and strong!

Color the leafy parts of these plants green to discover some of the foods that veggie dinosaurs ate.

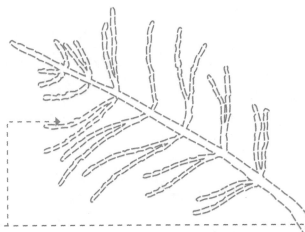

Cycads
These small trees and plants had woody stems and tough, spiky leaves that were hard to munch.

Conifers
Conifers such as pine trees, firs, and monkey puzzle trees had small green needles. Long-necked sauropods stripped them from the branches with their teeth.

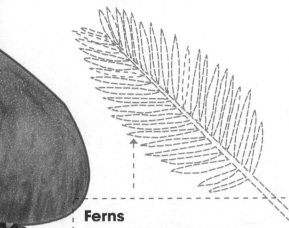

Ferns
These leafy green plants were low-growing, so they could be eaten by small veggie dinosaurs, too.

Horsetails
These plants grew in damp, marshy areas. They had straight, hollow stems, with circles of thin leaves growing around them.

Following the herd

Huge sauropods, such as *Diplodocus*, roamed together in herds. This gave them protection from large predators. But smaller animals also saw these giants as dinner!

It's like a modern-day mosquito!

Blood-drinking insects could have pierced the tough skin of a *Diplodocus* for a meal of blood.

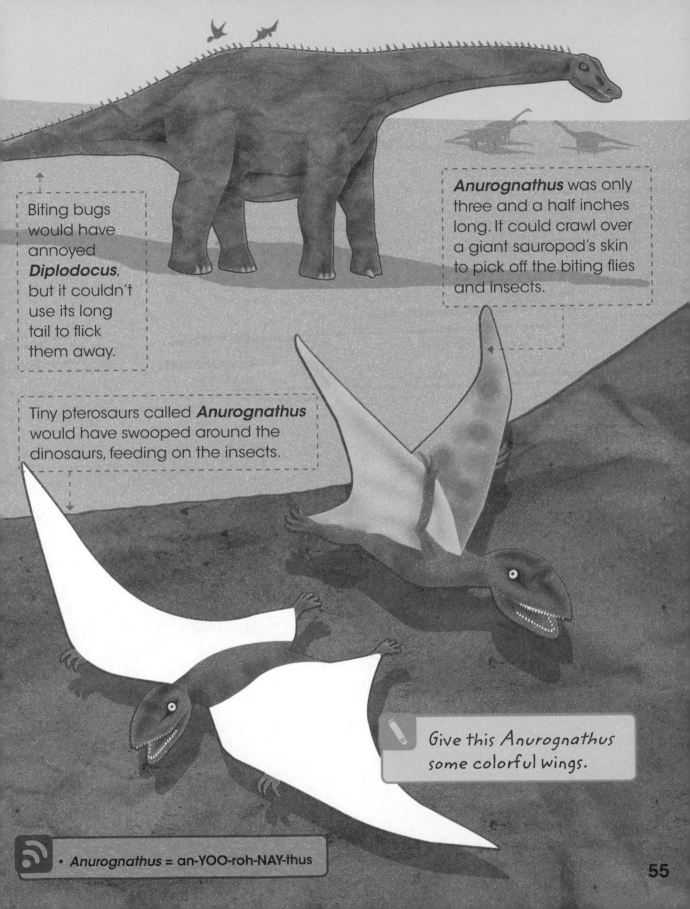

Biting bugs would have annoyed **Diplodocus**, but it couldn't use its long tail to flick them away.

Anurognathus was only three and a half inches long. It could crawl over a giant sauropod's skin to pick off the biting flies and insects.

Tiny pterosaurs called **Anurognathus** would have swooped around the dinosaurs, feeding on the insects.

Give this Anurognathus some colorful wings.

• *Anurognathus* = an-YOO-roh-NAY-thus

Furry mammals

The next stop for your time machine is the Middle Jurassic, about 165 million years ago. Dinosaurs still ruled, but a new type of animal was scurrying around, too.

A

Mammals have been around since the Triassic, but *Juramaia* were the first modern mammals. They were smaller than a modern-day mouse.

Most mammals give birth to live babies—they don't lay eggs like dinosaurs and other reptiles.

B

Juramaia had lots of tiny teeth and probably ate insects.

Mammals provide milk for their young and care for them until they can care for themselves.

Mammals have fur or hair. **Juramaia** had fur to keep its body warm. It hunted at night, when there were fewer predators.

C

Juramaia moved fast to avoid being eaten by dinosaurs and lizards.

D

E

• Juramaia = JOOR-ah-MY-ah

? Can you spot the two Juramaia that are exactly the same?

Early birds

Next stop, the Jurassic treetops! Take a look at the first known flying bird—*Archaeopteryx*. You'll see it's very different to the birds you can spot in your yard!

Archaeopteryx had claws on its wings for grasping branches and climbing trees.

Unlike modern birds, it had sharp teeth for snapping up insects and small reptiles.

Feathers helped to keep *Archaeopteryx* warm and were used for flying.

Beneath the feathers, *Archaeopteryx* had bones inside its long tail.

Archaeopteryx ran along the ground to chase its prey.

Find a route to help this Archaeopteryx catch its prey.

FINISH

START

• Archaeopteryx = AR-kee-OP-tr-iks

59

Fuzzy feathers

Did you know that fossils of nonflying dinosaurs with feathers have been discovered? The feathers of these dinos were quite simple and very different from those of modern-day birds.

Sciurumimus was a two-legged meat-eater. It was covered in thin fibers that looked like fur, but were actually simple feathers.

Get creative and color in *Sciurumimus's* bushy tail feathers.

The feathers were longest at the tail, making it look bushy like a squirrel's tail.

There may be many more feathered dinosaurs that have yet to be discovered.

Juravenator was a small two-legged meat-eater. It had long, simple feathers along the top of its back, hips, and tail.

Color in Juravenator's feathery coat.

They were not like bird feathers, but more like a fluffy coat.

Doodle a new dino with fancy feathers. Give your new discovery a name!

My feathery dinosaur is called

....

Anchiornis

Short, downy feathers all over its body kept **Anchiornis** warm and dry. Water ran off its feathers like on a waterproof raincoat!

DINO FACT FILE

 Say: an-KEE-or-nis

 Meaning of name: near bird

 Length: 13 inches

 Diet: meat, insects

 Lived: 161 to 151 million years ago

 Found in: China

The colorful, feathery crest might have helped to attract a mate or to warn other **Anchiornis** to keep away.

Scientists have figured out what color its feathers were. I can see they were right!

Anchiornis's front legs had developed into wings, but it couldn't fly like a bird. It's possible that it glided from the treetops down to the ground.

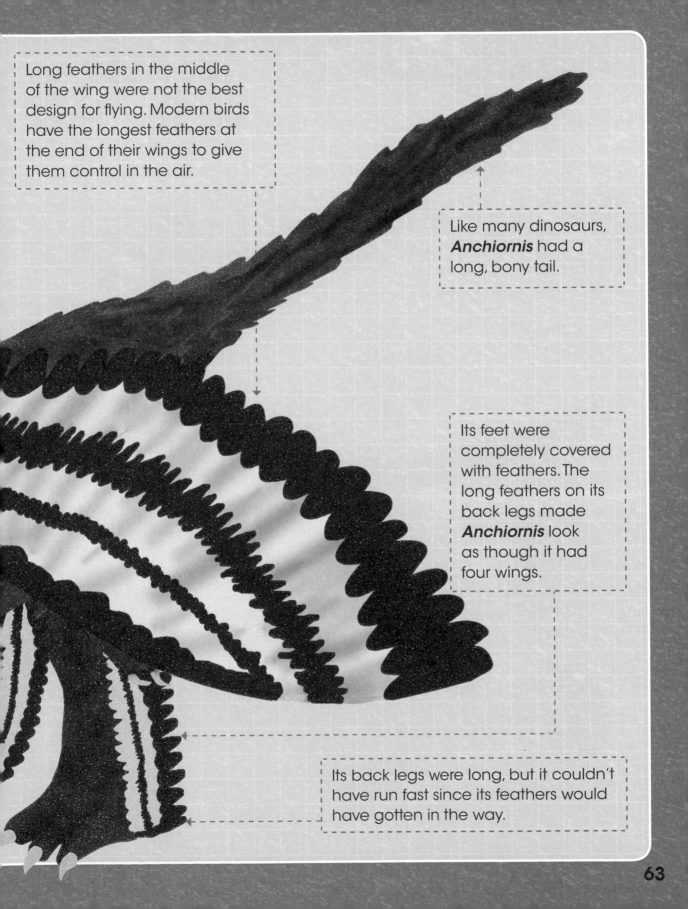

Long feathers in the middle of the wing were not the best design for flying. Modern birds have the longest feathers at the end of their wings to give them control in the air.

Like many dinosaurs, *Anchiornis* had a long, bony tail.

Its feet were completely covered with feathers. The long feathers on its back legs made *Anchiornis* look as though it had four wings.

Its back legs were long, but it couldn't have run fast since its feathers would have gotten in the way.

Dinosaur or bird?

Anchiornis may have looked like a bird, but under those feathers it was a dinosaur! Take a closer look at the hidden differences between *Anchiornis* and modern-day birds.

Dinosaur: *Anchiornis*

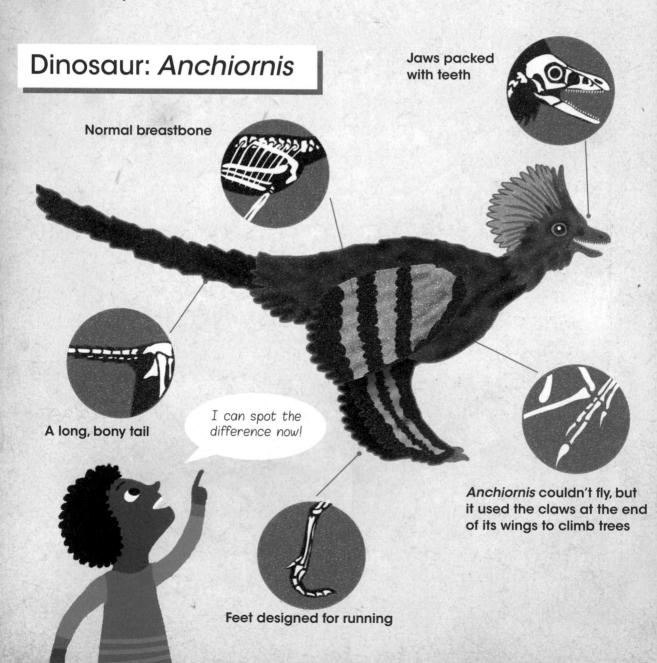

Jaws packed with teeth

Normal breastbone

A long, bony tail

I can spot the difference now!

Feet designed for running

Anchiornis couldn't fly, but it used the claws at the end of its wings to climb trees

Modern bird: Pigeon

Wings without claws

Most modern-day birds have a beak and no teeth

Short tail bones

Sturdy breastbone to attach wing muscles for flying

Feet designed for takeoff and landing, not for running. Modern-day birds are born to fly!

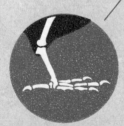

Now that you know the differences between *Anchiornis* and modern birds, try this True or False quiz!

1. Modern-day birds have claws on their wings.
TRUE FALSE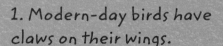

2. *Anchiornis* had jaws with teeth, rather than a beak.
TRUE FALSE

3. Modern-day birds have long, bony tails.
TRUE FALSE

4. *Anchiornis* could fly really well.
TRUE FALSE

5. Most modern-day birds don't have teeth.
TRUE FALSE

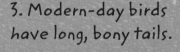

Hot and cold

Reptiles, such as lizards, are cold-blooded. This means that they need the heat of the sun to keep warm and active. It is likely that many dinosaurs were warm-blooded instead.

Warm-blooded animals keep their body temperature the same, even when it's very hot or very cold outside.

Small dinosaurs would have used some of the food they ate just to keep their bodies warm.

About 90 percent of the food we eat provides the energy to keep our bodies warm.

Humans, like all mammals, are warm-blooded.

Gargoyleosauru

- *Gargoyleosaurus* = GAR-goyle-oh-SORE-us
- *Fruitafossor* = FROO-ta-foss-or

To cool down, small dinosaurs, such as *Gargoyleosaurus*, would have moved into the shade.

The large bodies of giant dinosaurs would have taken a long time to heat up or cool down, so they were less affected by temperature changes throughout the day.

Mammals had fur or hair to help keep them warm. Some dinosaurs had feathers to stop them losing heat.

Being warm-blooded meant that small mammals, such as *Fruitafossor*, could sleep during the day and hunt at night, when it was cooler.

Stegosaurus

DINO FACT FILE

 Say: STEG-oh-SORE-us

 Meaning of name: roof lizard

 Length: 29 feet

 Diet: plants

 Lived: 156 to 145 million years ago

 Found in: United States

All dinosaurs had small brains, but *Stegosaurus* had a truly tiny brain—it was about the size of a walnut!

Steg's brain weighed 100,000 times less than its body, but that doesn't mean it was a dumb dino.

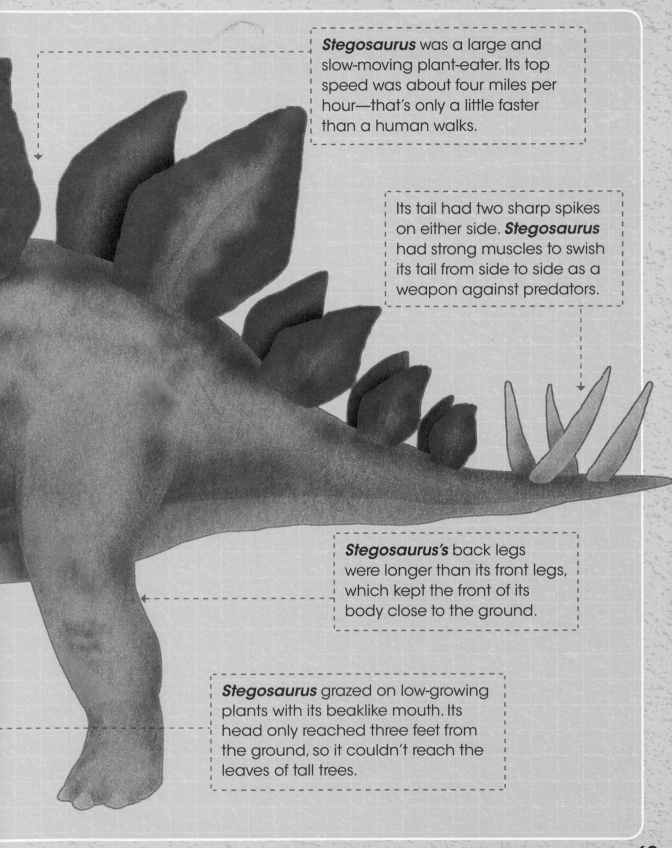

Stegosaurus was a large and slow-moving plant-eater. Its top speed was about four miles per hour—that's only a little faster than a human walks.

Its tail had two sharp spikes on either side. **Stegosaurus** had strong muscles to swish its tail from side to side as a weapon against predators.

Stegosaurus's back legs were longer than its front legs, which kept the front of its body close to the ground.

Stegosaurus grazed on low-growing plants with its beaklike mouth. Its head only reached three feet from the ground, so it couldn't reach the leaves of tall trees.

Colorful critters

Yikes! Your time machine has landed you in the middle of a herd of *Stegosaurus*. Take a look at the bony plates on their backs, but don't get too close to their spiky tails!

Stegosaurus had two rows of bony plates along its back and tail.

The plates helped *Stegosaurus* to control its body temperature. They soaked up heat from the sun to warm it up or cooled it down when a breeze blew over them.

A male *Stegosaurus* might have used its colorful plates to show off—either to attract a girlfriend or to frighten off a rival.

Steg's plates work best for showing off if they are really colorful! Color them in using your brightest colors.

Thankfully, Stegosaurus was a plant-eater!

Sea monsters

Time to make a splash and explore the deep, dark oceans of the Jurassic. By this time, some sea reptiles had become truly gigantic.

These sea monsters are not actually dinosaurs—they're all reptiles.

Just as land reptiles grew bigger in the Jurassic, so did sea reptiles. Giant plesiosaurs swam in the ocean depths.

Plesiosaurs had a streamlined shape to help them speed through the water.

Plesiosaurs had developed from land reptiles and still needed to breathe air.

Liopleurodon was a pliosaur—a type of plesiosaur with a large head and a short neck. Its strong jaws had long, snaggly teeth for catching large prey —even sharks and other plesiosaurs!

Smaller plesiosaurs such as *Microcleidus* had long necks and small heads—perfect for poking into small hiding places to snap up fish.

? Check off these other Jurassic sea creatures as you spot them.

Ammonite ○   Starfish ○

Jellyfish ○

Quick! Snap a photo of *Liopleurodon* for our travel blog!

Predator X

Pliosaurs such as *Liopleurodon* were about 20 feet long. But one colossal sea reptile, a pliosaur known as *Predator X*, grew up to 40 feet long!

 Connect the dots to reveal the biggest and scariest Jurassic sea monster!

Its head was six feet long—that's the height of a tall man.

It's time to get out of here!

TIME TOURS

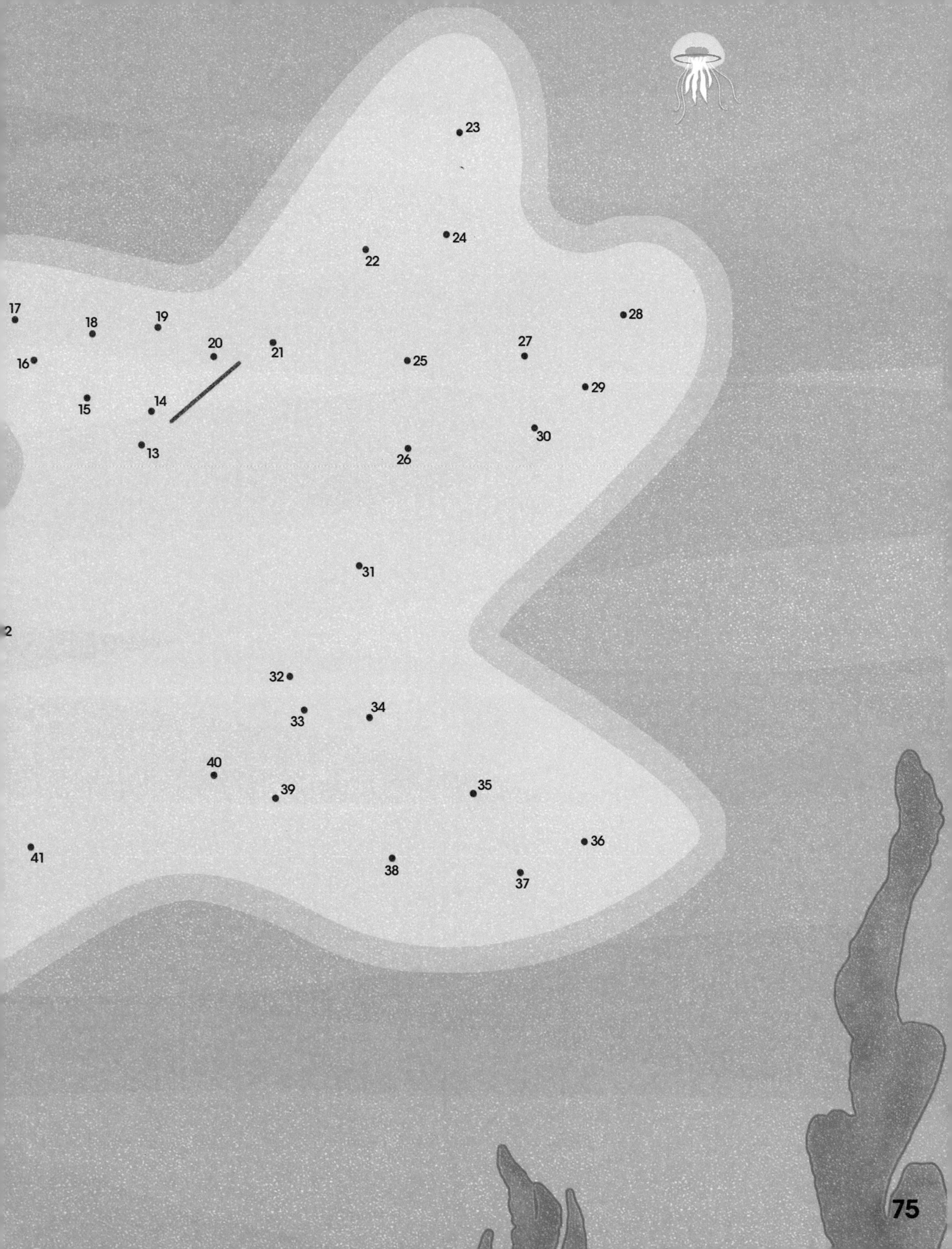

23

24

22

17

18   19

16   20   21   28

27

14   25

15   29

13   26   30

31

2

32

33   34

40

39   35

41   36

38   37

75

Allosaurus

Allosaurus was the largest predator of the Jurassic. It was as tall as a modern-da giraffe and tough enough to hunt giant *Diplodocus* o super-spiky *Stegosaurus.*

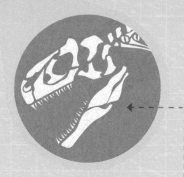

Its jaws were packed with pointed teeth that had jagged edges like a saw. They curved backward, making it impossible for prey to wriggle free.

Its hands had three curved claws for grasping and ripping into prey.

Yikes! Allosaurus's teeth were two to four inches long!

DINO FACT FILE

 Say: AL-oh-SORE-us

 Meaning of name: other lizard

 Length: 40 feet

 Diet: meat

 Lived: 156 to 144 million years ago

 Found in: Tanzania, United States

Allosaurus held its body in a straight line as it ran on its two back legs. Its tail helped it to balance as it ran.

Allosaurus's huge back legs were three times as long as its short front arms.

Allosaurus's teeth sometimes fell out as it shook its prey from side to side, but new teeth soon replaced them.

Its powerful muscles meant that *Allosaurus* could run at speeds of 20 miles per hour—faster than all but the best athletes.

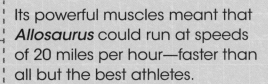

Puck lunch

Allosaurus was big, but some of the dinosaurs it liked to eat were even bigger! To bring down a huge *Diplodocus*, a group of *Allosaurus* may have hunted as a pack, sharing the meal afterward.

Let's get out of here—we don't want to be dessert!

Join the pack by drawing in your own fearsome *Allosaurus* here!

Diplodocus traveled in herds for protection, but the young and the sickly were a target for predators, especially if they strayed from the herd.

Cretaceous world

During the Cretaceous period, the world became warmer. Sea levels rose, and the continents we know today began to form. Dinosaurs continued to rule the world!

LAURASIA

GONDWANA

The landmasses of Laurasia and Gondwana broke up, and new continents slowly formed.

The dinosaurs on each new landmass developed to suit the conditions there.

In the Cretaceous, flowering plants appeared for the first time.

They provided extra food for plant-eating dinosaurs.

• *Gobisaurus* = GO-bee-SORE-us

Conifers and monkey puzzle trees were common in the Cretaceous, but leafy trees also began to grow.

Gobisaurus

Rain fell over the mountains, and shallow inland seas flooded low-lying areas. There was more water inland than during earlier times.

With flowers, plants started to get colorful. Make these flowers any colors you like!

Scary claws

Some Cretaceous dinosaurs had long, sharp claws. For predators, claws were a deadly weapon used for hunting, but plant-eating dinosaurs had claws, too. They may have used them for defense or to strip bark and leaves off trees.

Therizinosaurus

Therizinosaurus was a 32-foot-long plant-eating dinosaur. Standing on its back legs, it would have towered over many smaller dinosaurs.

Therizinosaurus had awesome long claws!

Its short arms had three claws. Each was almost three feet long—the longest claws of any dinosaur.

Let's keep our distance in case he forgets he's a plant-eater!

• *Therizinosaurus* = thair-uh-ZEEN-uh-SORE-us • *Velociraptor* = veh-loss-i-RAP-tor

 Connect the dots to complete this deadly *Velociraptor* claw.

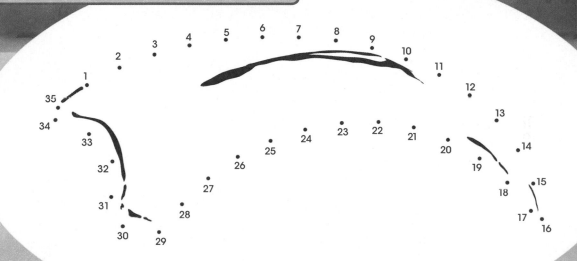

These straight, swordlike claws would have helped it to scare away predators or to fight them off!

Even though *Velociraptor* was not much bigger than a modern-day turkey, it was a fierce predator.

Velociraptor

Velociraptor used its claws to stab or tear at its prey. It could hold its extra-long foot claws out of the way while it ran.

Velociraptor had an extra-long curved claw, two and a half inches long on each foot.

83

Gone fishing

The rivers, lakes, and shallow seas of the Cretaceous were filled with fish. Lurking near the edges of the water were fish-eating dinos, such as *Baryonyx* and *Iguanadon*.

Baryonyx had a large thumb claw, nearly 10 inches long. It might have used this to stab fish or to hook them out of the water.

Baryonyx

 Draw more fish for these hungry dinos to catch.

Lepidotes

Lepidotes was a fish that was commonly found in Cretaceous waters. It was about a foot long.

Cretaceous fishes had bony scales, so these dinosaurs had to have strong teeth!

It had 96 super-sharp teeth to clamp onto prey such as slippery fish.

Baryonyx had a long and narrow snout, similar to that of a modern crocodile.

Iguanodon

Iguanodon also lived near the water and might have caught fish to eat, too.

85

Spinosaurus

Spinosaurus had long spines along its back. These probably held up a sail-like ridge of skin.

Spinosaurus was the largest-ever predator on land!

This giant weighed about one and a half times as much as an elephant!

DINO FACT FILE

 Say: SPY-nuh-SORE-us

 Meaning of name: spine lizard

 Length: 50 feet

 Diet: meat and fish

 Lived: 95 million years ago

 Found in: northern Africa

Spinosaurus's nostrils were high up on the snout, so it could keep its mouth underwater for a long time.

It lived on land and hunted along rivers. Its long snout was good for snatching fish out of the water.

Its jaws were packed with long, pointed teeth.

Spinosaurus didn't just eat fish. It also hunted on land or ate dead animals that it found. It was big enough to steal food from smaller predators, too.

The three claws on its hands were deadly, particularly the long thumb claw.

Showy Spinosaurus

Spinosaurus had a giant sail along its back. It was also six feet tall, so this dino really stood out. It might have been very colorful, too.

How will you color Spinosaurus? Do you want your dino to blend in with the background to creep up on prey, or to stand out to attract a mate?

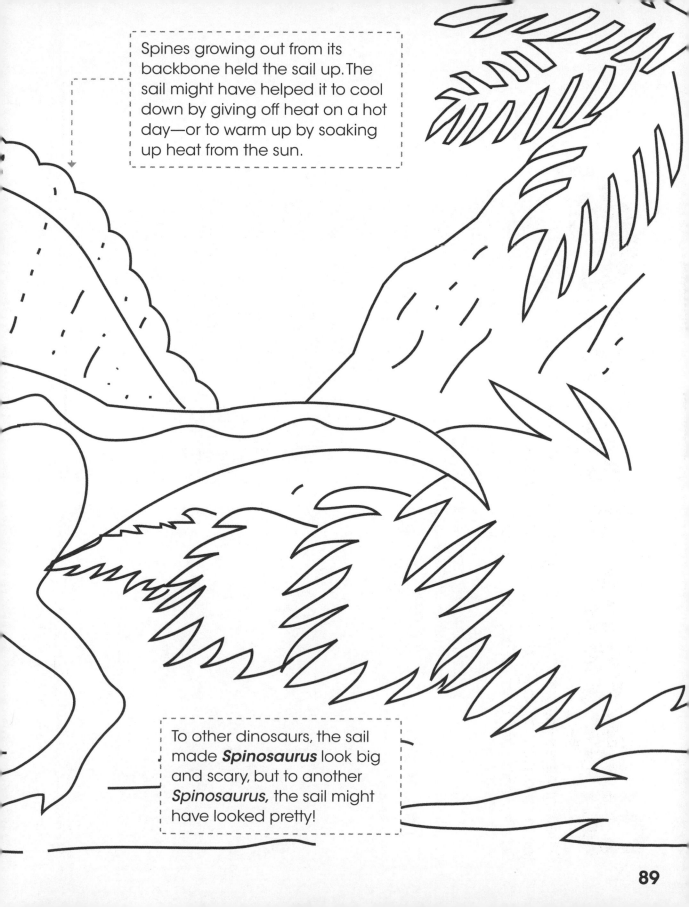

Spines growing out from its backbone held the sail up. The sail might have helped it to cool down by giving off heat on a hot day—or to warm up by soaking up heat from the sun.

To other dinosaurs, the sail made **Spinosaurus** look big and scary, but to another **Spinosaurus,** the sail might have looked pretty!

Dinosaur dentist

Different types of dinosaur had different kinds of teeth to deal with the type of food that they ate. Say "open wide" and take a closer look!

New T. rex teeth grew constantly from the bottom, replacing those that wore away or dropped out.

Tyrannosaurus rex

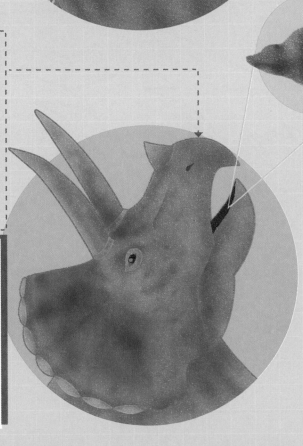

Tyrannosaurus rex had long, sharp teeth shaped like deadly bananas! A whole tooth could be nearly a foot long.

Like many plant-eating dinosaurs, *Triceratops* had a beak to clip through tough plants.

Triceratops

Farther back in its mouth were banks of up to 800 closely packed teeth. These were used to grind up the leaves and twigs it ate.

Alamosaurus used its teeth to rake the leaves off tree branches and ferns.

Alamosaurus was a giant sauropod that ate plants. It had teeth shaped like pegs.

Alamosaurus

Color the shapes the same as their colored dots to reveal T. rex's jaws.

Meat-eating dinos had had deadly teeth. *Troodon* had more than 100 small, needle-sharp teeth in its jaws.

Troodon

- *Triceratops* = try-SAIR-uh-tops · *Alamosaurus* = AL-uh-mo-SORE-us
- *Tyrannosaurus rex* = tie-RAN-uh-SORE-us recks · *Troodon* = TRO-uh-don

91

Ankylosaurus

DINO FACT FILE

 Say: ang-KYLE-uh-SORE-us

 Meaning of name: fused lizard

 Length: 32 feet

 Diet: plants

 Lived: 70 to 65 million years ago

 Found in: North America

Ankylosaurus had bony plates called scutes (say: scoots) over its body. They acted like a suit of armor to protect it from predators.

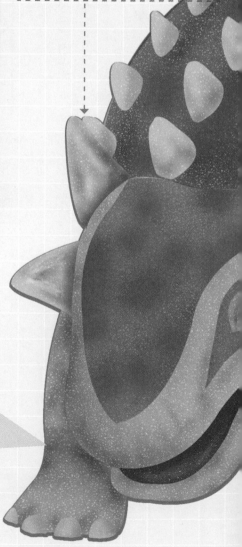

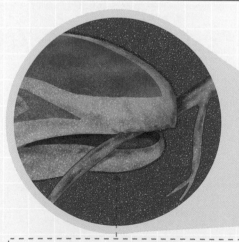

Ankylosaurus's wide beak was hard and sharp for biting through stems and roots. It had small triangular teeth farther back in its mouth for chewing tough plants.

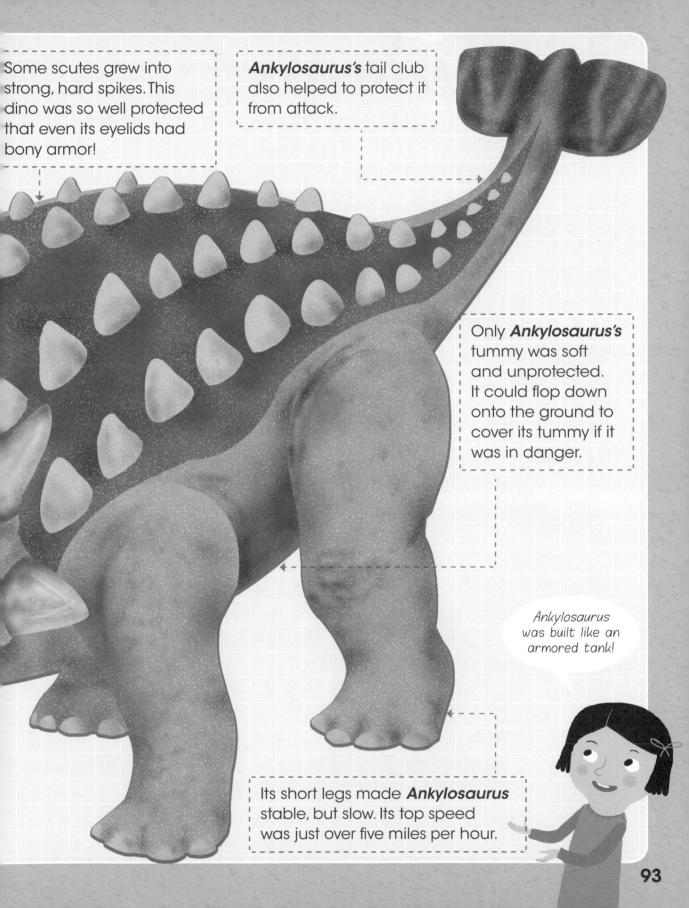

Some scutes grew into strong, hard spikes. This dino was so well protected that even its eyelids had bony armor!

Ankylosaurus's tail club also helped to protect it from attack.

Only *Ankylosaurus's* tummy was soft and unprotected. It could flop down onto the ground to cover its tummy if it was in danger.

Ankylosaurus was built like an armored tank!

Its short legs made *Ankylosaurus* stable, but slow. Its top speed was just over five miles per hour.

Tail defenses

With all those deadly predators around, plant-eaters needed protection. Many had body armor, spikes, or horns. Others, including *Ankylosaurus*, also had fearsome tail weapons.

Ankylosaurus—tail club

Ankylosaurus had a heavy club made of solid bone at the end of its tail. The tail bones were joined together to make a strong handle for swinging the club around.

CRUNCH!

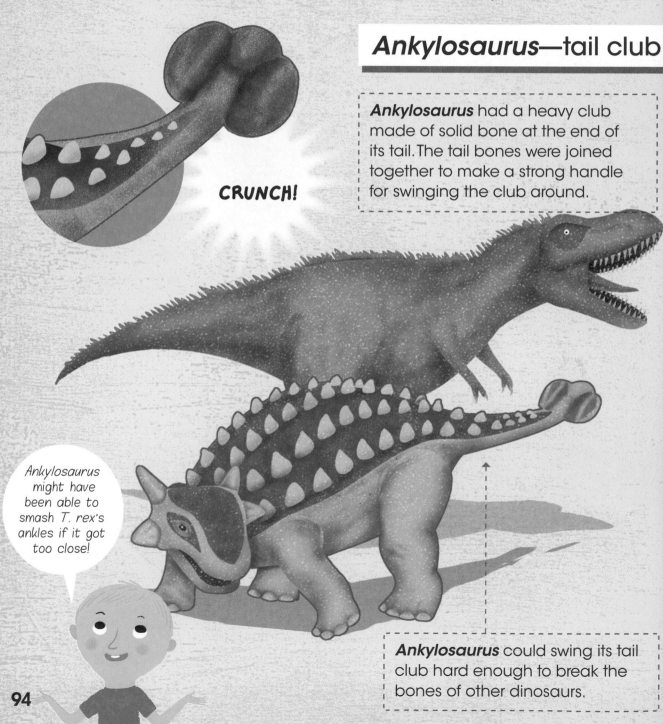

Ankylosaurus might have been able to smash T. rex's ankles if it got too close!

Ankylosaurus could swing its tail club hard enough to break the bones of other dinosaurs.

Swishing a deadly tail weapon about may have been enough to scare away most predators. Check out these other dino tail defenses.

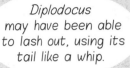
Diplodocus may have been able to lash out, using its tail like a whip.

Diplodocus—whip tail

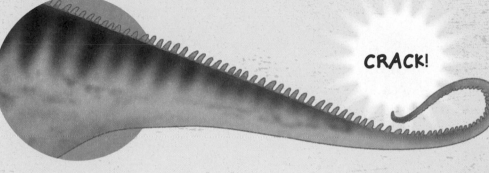

CRACK!

Stegosaurus—tail spikes

SLASH!

Stegosaurus had vicious spikes on the end of its tail.

Design your own dino tail weapon. Add spikes, saw-shaped blades, or even a giant sting!

Dino babies

All dinosaur babies hatched from eggs. Some eggs were the size of footballs; others were small enough to hold in your hand. The eggs had hard shells to protect the dinosaur babies inside.

Maiasaura were large plant-eating dinosaurs that lived in herds. They laid their eggs in nests built close together.

Maiasaura made nests by scraping holes in the ground or by making piles of earth, sand, and stones. The nests were round and held between 20 and 40 eggs.

When the babies hatched, their parents brought them berries and seeds to eat. The babies stayed in the nest while their parents looked after them.

The parents protected the eggs with a layer of leaves. They may even have sat on their nests to keep the eggs warm and safe.

The hatchlings were about 10 inches long.

• *Maiasaura* = mah-ee-ah-SORE-uh • *Bambiraptor* = BAM-bee-RAP-tore

Other dinosaurs ate eggs or hatchlings. **Maiasaura** parents had to guard against predators such as **Bambiraptor**.

FINISH

START

Can you find a route for this Maiasaura baby to get back to its nest?

Triceratops

DINO FACT FILE

 Say: try-SAIR-uh-tops

 Meaning of name: three-horned face

 Length: 30 feet

 Diet: plants

 Lived: 70 million years ago

 Found in: North America

Triceratops lived in large herds, just like elephants today. The males often fought—the strongest male could choose the best dino girlfriend!

Triceratops was just over six feet tall, but it was strong enough to push over trees to feed on all the tasty leaves.

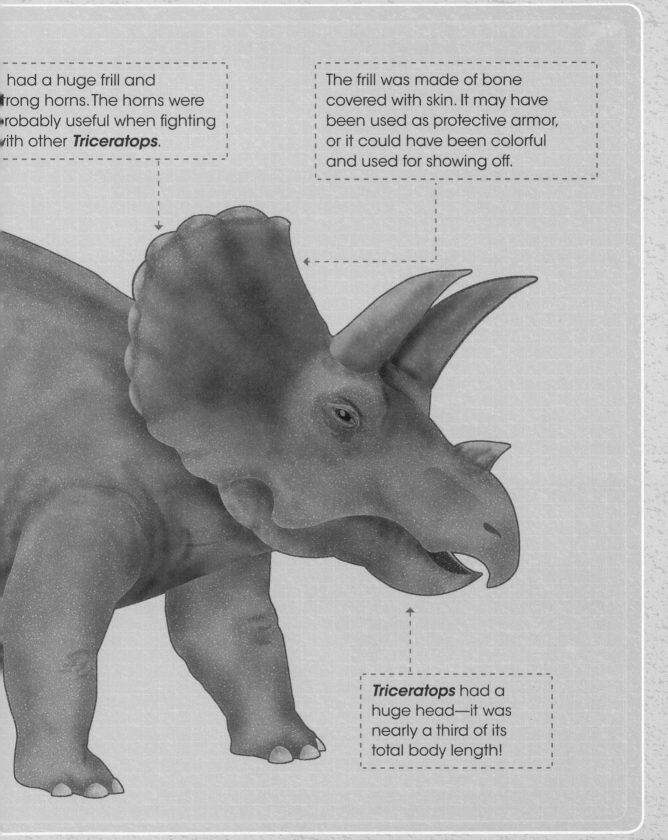

had a huge frill and
trong horns. The horns were
robably useful when fighting
with other *Triceratops*.

The frill was made of bone
covered with skin. It may have
been used as protective armor,
or it could have been colorful
and used for showing off.

Triceratops had a
huge head—it was
nearly a third of its
total body length!

99

Dino headgear

Triceratops's head frill made it look big and scary. The frill might have warned other dinosaurs not to attack, or it could have helped to attract a mate. Other dinos had fancy headgear, too.

The frill might have helped ***Triceratops*** to control its body temperature. It could have held the frill up to the wind to cool down, or to face the sun to warm up.

Styracosaurus had even more spikes than ***Triceratops***, with four to six long horns, plus a small horn on each cheek and another horn on its nose!

Triceratops had three horns. The two long horns above the eyes could grow up to three feet long.

Triceratops needed horns to protect it from predators, such as Tyrannosaurus rex.

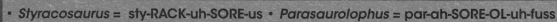

- ***Styracosaurus*** = sty-RACK-uh-SORE-us • ***Parasaurolophus*** = par-ah-SORE-OL-uh-fuss
- ***Pachycephalosaurus*** = pak-ee-SEF-uh-lo-SORE-us

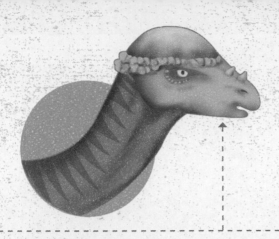 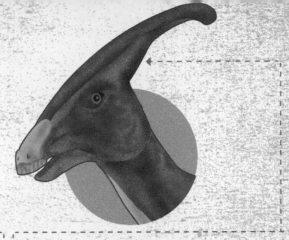

Pachycephalosaurus had a dome of bone 10 inches thick on top of its head. It was probably used for ramming into other **Pachycephalosaurus!**

Parasaurolophus had a long crest on its head. The crest was hollow and was used like a trumpet to make sounds.

 Use the left-hand side as a guide to complete this *Triceratops* and then give him a colorful frill.

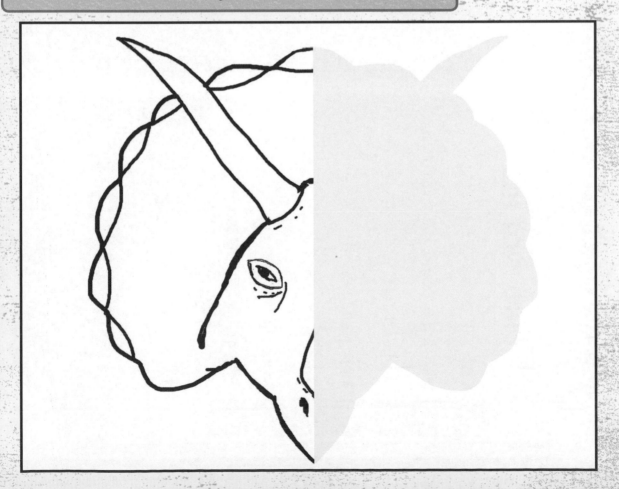

Tyrannosaurus rex

If you traveled in a time machine to North America 65 million years ago, you might have come face to face with *Tyrannosaurus rex*, one of the fiercest and deadliest predators to have ever lived.

DINO FACT FILE

 Say: tie-RAN-uh-SORE-us recks

Meaning of name: tyrant lizard king

 Length: 39 feet

 Diet: meat

 Lived: 70 to 65 million years ago

 Found in: North America

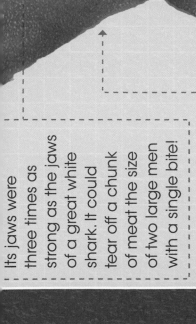

Tyrannosaurus rex had tiny arms that didn't even reach to its mouth. But they had powerful muscles and hooked claws that could have been used to hold struggling prey.

Tyrannosaurus rex weighed as much as a large elephant, but was taller and longer.

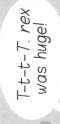

T-t-t-*T. rex* was huge!

Its jaws were three times as strong as the jaws of a great white shark. It could tear off a chunk of meat the size of two large men with a single bite!

Young tyrannosaurs grew slowly, but in their teens they put on about 1,300 pounds a year for several years—eating 20 to 30 pounds of meat a day! Adults weighed around 20,000 pounds.

A balancing act

Fossilized footprints suggest that *Tyrannosaurus rex* could move pretty fast. But how did *T. rex* manage to move around so quickly with that huge and heavy head?

Just like a seesaw!

It's all down to balance.

T. rex held its spine almost level with the ground when it walked or ran.

The tail was held off the ground to balance the huge weight of the head.

Fossil footprints suggest that *T. rex* could move pretty quickly, at almost 30 miles per hour.

Its two legs acted as a balance point.

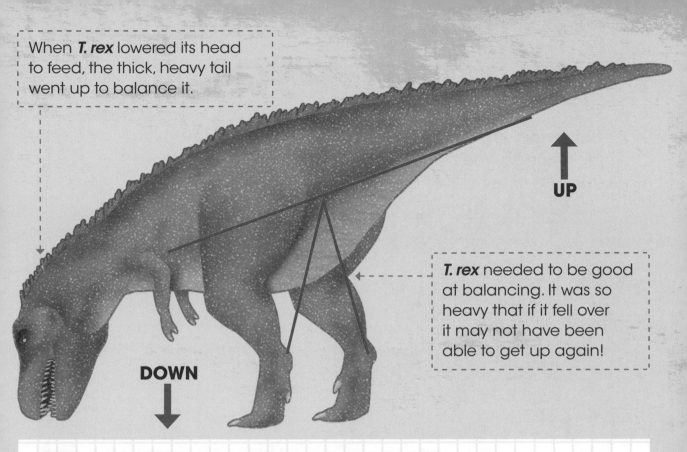

When **T. rex** lowered its head to feed, the thick, heavy tail went up to balance it.

UP

DOWN

T. rex needed to be good at balancing. It was so heavy that if it fell over it may not have been able to get up again!

✂ Make a model T. rex from modeling clay and lollipop sticks, and try this balancing experiment!

How long does the tail have to be to balance the head?

❶ Make an oval shape for the body, and stick two lollipop sticks into the middle for legs.

❸ Make a big round head and a long hotdog shape for the tail.

❷ Add feet and get your model to balance, so that it stands up by itself.

❹ Add more modeling clay to either end to see if you can get your T. rex to balance.

105

Noisy dinosaurs

Dinosaurs were very noisy! As well as stomping around, crashing through trees, and chomping on their food, some dinosaurs made noises or sounds to signal to each other.

Dinosaurs with long necks could make low, deep, sounds that carried a long way. *Alamosaurus* could call to each other over very long distances.

Dinosaurs like *Alamosaurus* traveled in herds as they looked for plants to munch. Calling to each other could have been a way to keep the herd together.

That's a big dino making a BIG noise!

I wish I'd brought some earplugs!

Corythosaurus had strange crests on their heads that they used to make honking sounds.

Inside the crests were hollow tubes they could blow through. The crests worked a little like built-in trumpets.

Gryposaurus's nose made hooting or snorting sounds that could attract a mate or warn about danger.

? Can you find ten musical notes hidden in this scene?

• *Corythosaurus* = ko-RITH-uh-SORE-us • *Gryposaurus* = GRYE-puh-SORE-us

Parasaurolophus

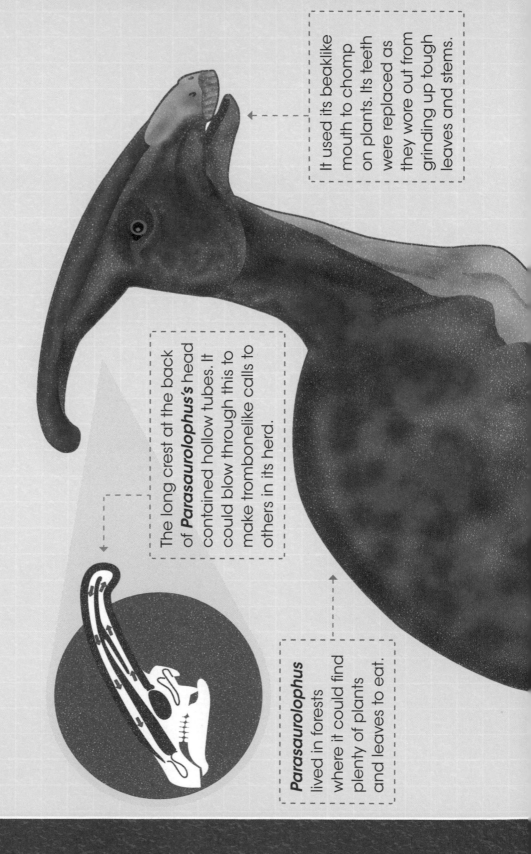

It used its beaklike mouth to chomp on plants. Its teeth were replaced as they wore out from grinding up tough leaves and stems.

The long crest at the back of *Parasaurolophus's* head contained hollow tubes. It could blow through this to make trombonelike calls to others in its herd.

Parasaurolophus lived in forests where it could find plenty of plants and leaves to eat.

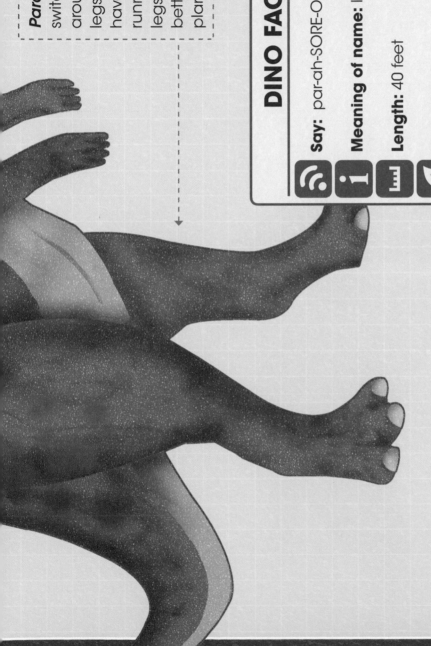

Parasaurolophus could switch between walking around on two or four legs. Two legs would have been used for running. Moving on four legs may have been better for feeding on plants at ground level.

DINO FACT FILE

 Say: par-ah-SORE-OL-uh-fuss

 Meaning of name: like a crested lizard

Length: 40 feet

Diet: plants

 Lived: 76 to 65 million years ago

Found in: North America

Wow—that incredible crest was more than twice the length of its head!

High flyers

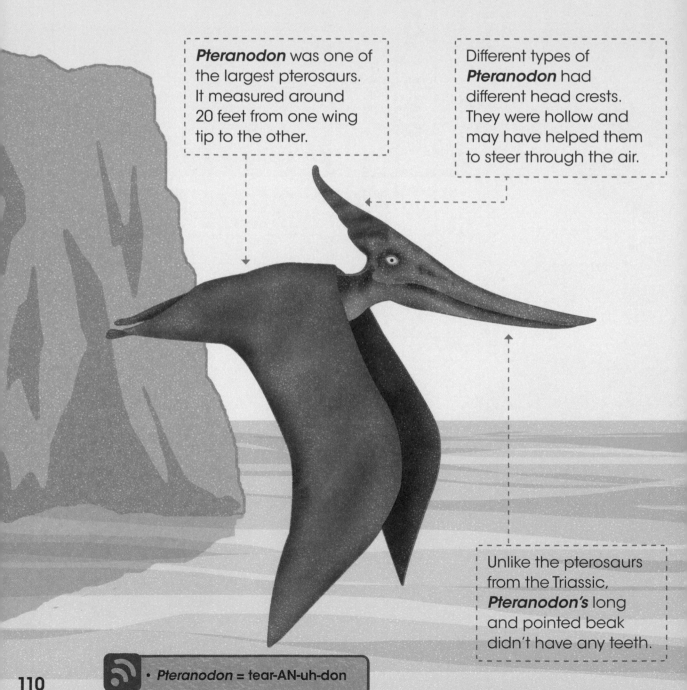

Is it a bird? Is it a plane? Neither—it's a flying reptile!
Huge pterosaurs flew through the Cretaceous skies.
They were much larger than pterosaurs from the Triassic.

Pteranodon was one of the largest pterosaurs. It measured around 20 feet from one wing tip to the other.

Different types of *Pteranodon* had different head crests. They were hollow and may have helped them to steer through the air.

Unlike the pterosaurs from the Triassic, *Pteranodon's* long and pointed beak didn't have any teeth.

• *Pteranodon* = tear-AN-uh-don

Nyctosaurus was
a much smaller
pterosaur, with
a wingspan of six
to ten feet.

 Give this Nyctosaurus
a colorful head crest.

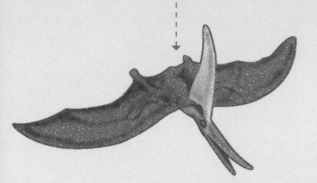

Its huge crest had a flap of skin
stretched like a sail between two
bones in an L-shape. This crest
made it attractive to a mate
and may have helped it to fly.

Both **Pteranodon** and
Nyctosaurus lived
close to the sea, where
they swooped down to
catch fish to eat.

 • *Nyctosaurus* = NICK-toe-SORE-us

Giants of the skies

The largest of the pterosaurs was the flying giant, **Quetzalcoatlus**. Twice the size of *Pteranodon*, it had a wingspan as wide as that of a small airplane!

Its long neck was about 10 feet long and the head had a large crest.

Quetzalcoatlus had a long, toothless beak. It may have fed on fish from inland lakes or on dead land animals—a bit like a modern-day vulture, but much bigger!

On the ground, **Quetzacoatlus** was as tall as a giraffe! It walked on its back feet, using its folded wings as front legs.

• *Quetzalcoatlus* = KWET-zell-KWAT-lus

Its vast wings were used to glide on rising warm air currents. It's possible that **Quetzalcoatlus** could have stayed in the air for up to a week!

Quetzacoatlus could fly at an incredibly speedy 80 miles an hour!

Color the shapes the same color as their dots to see how big Quetzalcoatlus looked!

Velociraptor

Velociraptor's jaws had a bite as strong as that of a modern-day lion.

DINO FACT FILE

 Say: veh-loss-i-RAP-tor

 Meaning of name: speedy thief

 Length: 6 feet

 Diet: meat

 Lived: 85 to 80 million years ago

 Found in: Asia

Velociraptor's teeth were widely spaced and had rough edges that would have cut through flesh like a saw!

Its body was covered with feathers, but *Velociraptor* couldn't fly. The feathers may have been used for display or to help keep its body warm.

Feather patterns might have helped *Velociraptors* to recognize each other.

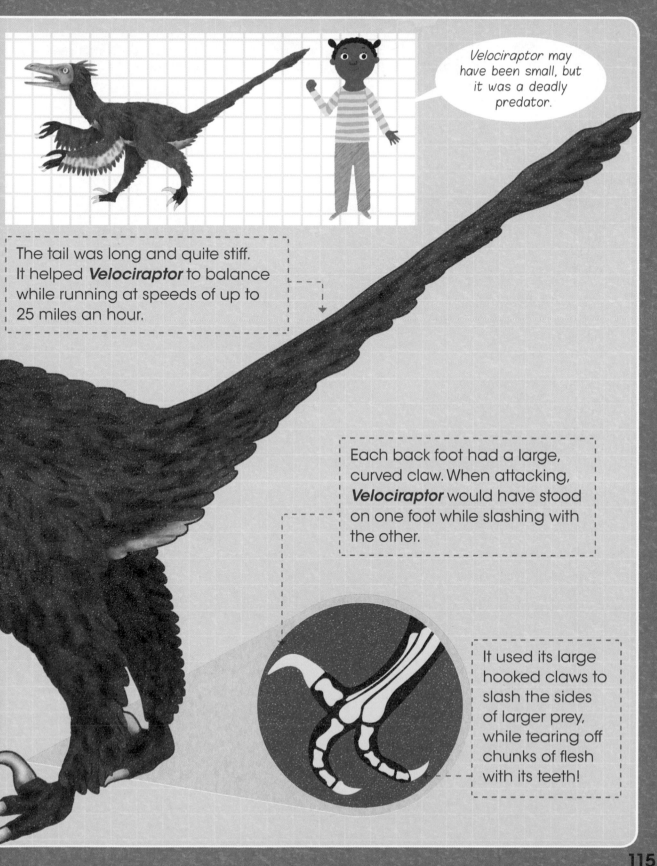

Velociraptor may have been small, but it was a deadly predator.

The tail was long and quite stiff. It helped **Velociraptor** to balance while running at speeds of up to 25 miles an hour.

Each back foot had a large, curved claw. When attacking, **Velociraptor** would have stood on one foot while slashing with the other.

It used its large hooked claws to slash the sides of larger prey, while tearing off chunks of flesh with its teeth!

The last of the dinosaurs

The sky filled with dust and smoke that darkened the sun for years.

Dinosaurs roamed the Earth for an incredible 180 million years, but then catastrophe struck! Take a trip back 65 million years to discover why there are no dinosaurs today.

A giant asteroid—a huge rock hurtling through space—crashed into Earth. The rock was the size of a city!

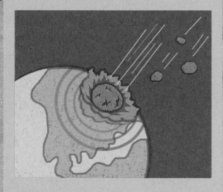

It smashed into the sea near modern-day Mexico, creating massive waves that flooded the land.

Quick! Get back in the time machine. Let's head home to the future—FAST!

TIME TOURS

More than half the types of animal on Earth were wiped out. This included all the larger animals, such as the dinosaurs.

A wave of heat from the crash started fires all over the planet.

Plants died without sunlight, and then the animals that ate the plants died, which meant the animals that ate the plant-eaters died.

With the dinosaurs gone, the world was taken over by new animals—mammals, which in the future led to humans like you!

Fust forward

It's time to go home, back to the present day.
Make a couple of short stops along the way to
check out what happened after the dinosaurs.

25 million years ago

With the large land reptiles out
of the way, mammals and birds
became the most important
species on Earth.

Vast areas of
grassland appeared,
and new species
of plant-eating
mammals fed on it,
including giants such
as *Deinotherium*.

New and unusual meat-eaters
appeared, too, including huge
pigs such as *Enteledon*.

Deinotherium was three times the size of a modern-day elephant!

TIME TOURS

It's only another 25 million years until we get home!

Miohippus was a three-toed prehistoric horse that grazed on the grasslands.

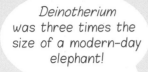 Write a prehistoric postcard before you get home. What was the most amazing thing you saw on your trip?

To: _____

_____

_____

_____

- *Deinotherium* = DYE-no-THEE-ree-um   • *Enteledon* = en-TELL-oh-don
- *Miohippus* = MY-oh-HIP-us

Almost home

Just 10,000 years to get back to the present day. But the world is still very different and filled with strange animals. Some of the newcomers look strangely familiar . . . .

10,000 years ago

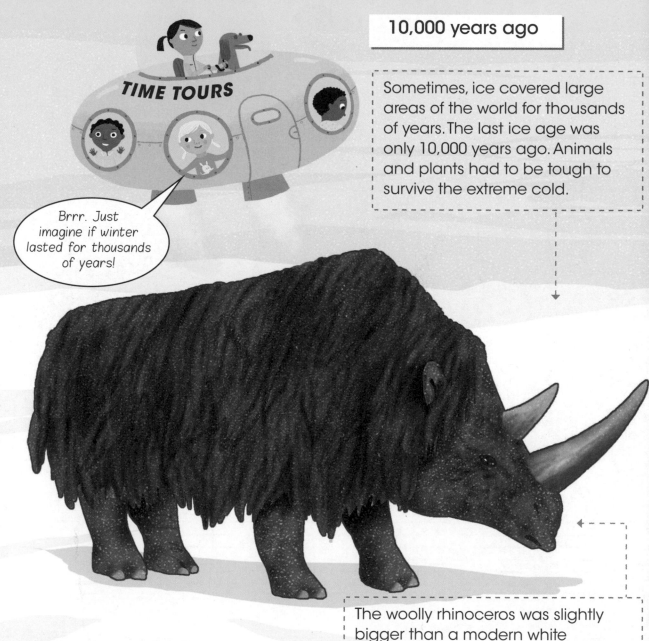

Sometimes, ice covered large areas of the world for thousands of years. The last ice age was only 10,000 years ago. Animals and plants had to be tough to survive the extreme cold.

Brrr. Just imagine if winter lasted for thousands of years!

The woolly rhinoceros was slightly bigger than a modern white rhinoceros. It had two tough horns for defense against predators.

Early humans lived at this time. They hunted animals, such as woolly mammoths and woolly rhinos, for food. They used their bones for tools and made clothes out of their skins.

Hey! I think I just spotted some of our human ancestors down there!

TIME TOURS

The woolly mammoth was about the same size as a modern African elephant, but it had much longer curved tusks.

Finding fossils

Although the dinosaurs died, they didn't disappear without a trace. Whenever a dinosaur body got buried, there was a small chance that it might be turned into a fossil.

When a dead animal becomes a fossil, its remains turn slowly to stone. Often, the fossil bones are all scrambled up when they are discovered.

Usually only the hard parts of a dinosaur, such as its bones, survive as fossils.

Some rare fossils have impressions of skin or feathers.

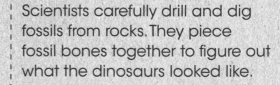

Scientists carefully drill and dig fossils from rocks. They piece fossil bones together to figure out what the dinosaurs looked like.

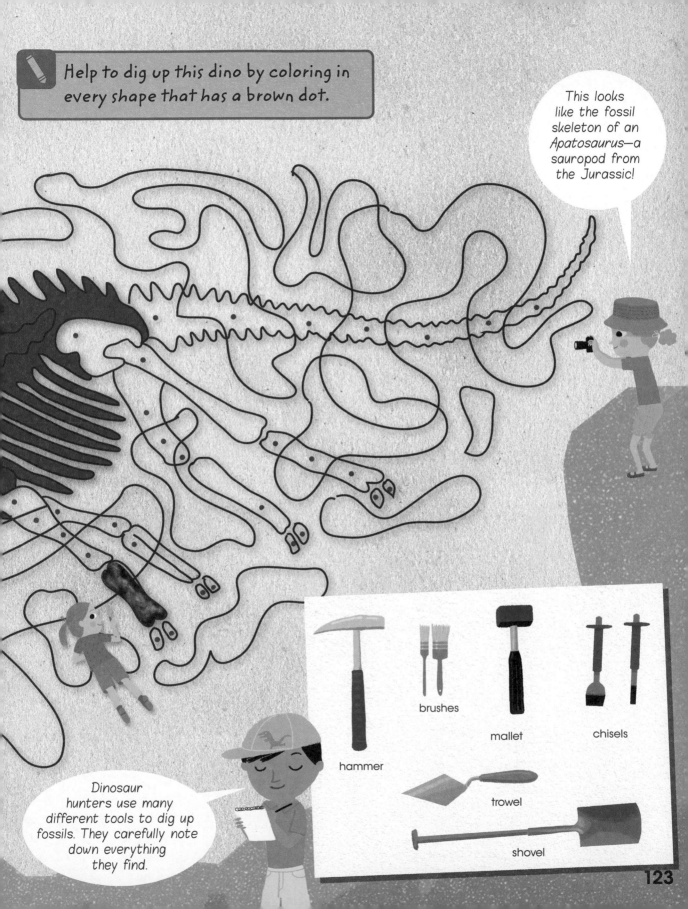

Glossary

Check out the meaning of lots of amazing dinosaur words right here!

Acid rain When some chemical gases are released into the air, they can react with it to make acidic rainfall. Such gases can be released by volcanoes. Acid rain can be harmful and even deadly to plant and animal life.

Amphibians These are cold-blooded animals without scaly skin, that can live in water or on land. Examples of modern-day amphibians are frogs and salamanders.

Camouflage The color, pattern, or shape of an animal that helps it to blend in with its surroundings.

Carnivore A class of animals that feeds on the flesh of other animals.

Cretaceous A period of time that lasted about 80 million years, spanning from 145 to 66 million years ago. The Cretaceous period was the last part of an even more incredibly huge span of time called the Mesozoic era.

Dinosaurs A group of land reptiles that lived on Earth millions of years ago. More than 700 different types of dinosaur have been discovered so far.

Extinct An animal becomes extinct when there are no living examples of it anywhere in the world.

Fossils The remains of plants and animals or traces left by them, such as footprints, which have been preserved in rocks.

Herbivore A class of animals that doesn't feed on flesh, but that eats only vegetable or plant matter. Cows are modern-day herbivores.

Jurassic The Jurassic period was the middle part of the Mesozoic era and lasted from 201 to 145 million years ago.

Lava The hot, molten rock from beneath the Earth's crust becomes lava when it reaches the surface—for example, when it flows out of a volcano during an eruption.

Lizard A type of reptile that usually has scaly skin, a tail, and four legs that splay out sideways from its long body. Geckos are modern-day lizards.

Mammals Warm-blooded animals with fur or hair, that produce milk to feed their babies. Human beings are mammals—so are dogs and dolphins.

Mesozoic The Mesozoic was a vast span of time, known as an era. It lasted from over 252 million years ago until 66 million years ago. The rise and fall of the dinosaurs happened over millions of years within the Mesozoic era.

Mass extinction The dying out, or extinction, of a large number of different types of living things in a relatively short period of time. A mass extinction is usually caused by a disaster, such as volcanic activity on a global scale.

Omnivore A type of animal that gets energy from eating both the flesh of other animals and plants or vegetables. Humans are modern-day omnivores— so are pigs.

Pangaea The huge single landmass that existed before and during the Triassic period. All the continents were joined together to form this one supercontinent.

Panthalassa The massive global ocean that surrounded the supercontinent Pangaea millions of years ago.

Predator A meat-eating animal that hunts and kills other animals to eat. The animals it hunts are known as prey.

Reptiles Cold-blooded animals that have backbones and dry, scaly skin, and that lay eggs on land. Dinosaurs were a type of reptile. Snakes, lizards, crocodiles, turtles, and tortoises are all types of reptile that are alive today.

Scales Tough, overlapping plates that cover and protect the skin of reptiles and fish. Dinosaurs had scaly skin, too.

Triassic The first period of the Mesozoic era lasting from 252 to 201 million years ago. During this huge span of time, the first dinosaurs appeared.

Another wonderful fossil find for the museum!

125

Index

Answers

Page 6
1-True, 2-False, 3-False

Pages 10-11

Pages 12-13

Pages 18-19

Pages 22-23
There are six camouflaged dinosaurs to spot.

Pages 26-27

Pages 34-35

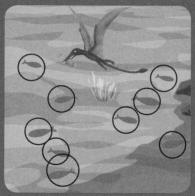

Pages 38-39
Only the ichthyosaurs survived into the Jurassic.

Pages 42-43
Stegosaurus-stegosaurs
Gargoyleosaurus-ankylosaurs
Allosaurus-theropods
Camptosaurus-cerapods
Apatosaurus-sauropods

Page 47
There are 22 theropod footprints.

Pages 56-57
Juramaia A and E are exactly the same.

Pages 58-59

Pages 64-65
1-False, 2-True, 3-False, 4-False, 5-True

Pages 90-91

Pages 96-97

Page 107

Page 113

128